P9-AGX-801

PRAISE FOR
PETER MOSKOS' *IN DEFENSE OF FLOGGING:*

"If we're capable of taking Moskos' idea as a serious option to incarceration, it could have profound consequences for a nation that incarcerates its citizens at a rate that's seven times as high as the other nations of the world. Clearly we have to find a way to reduce prison populations, and this just might be a logical one. . . . *In Defense of Flogging* forces the reader to confront issues surrounding incarceration that most Americans would prefer not to think about."
—*The Daily Beast*

"*In Defense of Flogging* is less a brief for the resumption of corporal punishment than an indictment of America's system of mass imprisonment. . . . Granted, flogging criminals would be ugly. But it would also make their punishment immediate and transparent. And it wouldn't be nearly as destructive and dysfunctional as keeping 2.3 million people in cages."
—*Boston Globe*

"With his provocatively titled new release, [Moskos] hopes to reinsert flogging and corporal punishment into the debate about the future of the prison system, one of America's most spectacularly failing institutions. . . . While the premise might seem outrageous, the book is well-timed. . . . The idea that caning hurts—a lot—but is quick and simple means it has the potential to bridge the divide between liberal prison reformists and hard-on-crime conservatives. Ultimately Moskos is on the same page as advocates for prison reform who point out the inefficiencies, racism, and lack of justice inherent in our current system." —*GOOD Magazine*

"Well-reasoned. . . . Even if you aren't convinced that flogging is the future, though, Moskos' deeper argument is still compelling. The act of punishment, he argues, is inherently strange, uncomfortable, and unsettling; there's a natural impulse to hide it away. Our prison system, though, shows that this is a mistake. . . . Instead of piling on the prison terms, we need to start asking hard questions about the value and meaning of punishment. Until then, we'll never have a sensible prison system." —*Boston Globe*, Brainiac

"[An] elegant polemic." —*Maclean's*

"*In Defense of Flogging* isn't a joke, a satire, or a thought experiment. . . . [Moskos] makes a convincing case. . . . *In Defense of Flogging* is one of the very few public-policy books I've encountered that goes past wringing its hands over a societal problem to offer a viable solution, by which I mean one with a prayer of being put into place because it has appeal across the political spectrum. . . . At just over 150 pages of clear, smart, and highly readable prose, Moskos's sharp little volume has a potential audience far beyond the experts who dutifully slog through most tomes like this. It's the kind of item that could be stacked next to a bookstore's cash register. Think about it for a Fathers' Day gift. . . . I know one thing, though. Given the choice between 10 lashes and five years, I'd take the whip."
—Craig Seligman, *Bloomberg News*

"You rascal, I thought. Moskos . . . knows how to catch our attention. . . . Against that backdrop [of our prison system], Moskos' startling invitation to reconsider the whip, cane, and cat-o'-nine-tails doesn't sound so preposterous. At least it gets us thinking." —Clarence Page, *Chicago Tribune*

"As a former Baltimore City police officer [and] assistant professor of law, police science and criminal justice administration at John Jay College of Criminal Justice, Mr. Moskos is not unfamiliar with the legal or criminal aspects of justice. He readily employs this background to describe the ills of today's criminal justice system and his radical alternative. . . . *Flogging* is intriguing, even in—or because of—its shocking premise. As a case against prisons, Mr. Moskos' is airtight." —*Washington Times*

"Peter Moskos' *In Defense of Flogging* might seem like a satire—akin to Jonathan Swift's 'A Modest Proposal,' an essay advocating the eating of children—but it is as serious as a wooden stick lashing into a blood-splattered back." —Adam Cohen, Time.com

"Though its title suggests a Swiftian satire, this book by criminal justice professor Peter Moskos is a genuine call to reinstate flogging as a voluntary alternative to incarceration."
—*Mother Jones*, Favorite Book of 2011

"A way of vivifying what's wrong with the system we have now."
—*The Village Voice*

"Hardly a literal remedy, Moskos' slender monograph falls in the tradition of the modest proposal, a shocking solution selected to prick the public conscience by exposing some great social injustice."
—*News and Observer* (Raleigh, NC)

"*In Defense of Flogging* is a brilliant piece of work. It is well informed, shows command of the facts and relevant social research, challenges the reader to think about an important policy issue—America's exceptional large prison population—and is witty, entertaining, and creative. The time has come for Americans to have a discussion about America's failed penal system."
—Wendell Bell, Professor Emeritus of Sociology, Yale University

"Moskos's argument is moral, deeply felt, and deeply affecting, predicated on the belief that American citizens have a responsibility to 'open [our] eyes to our massive and horrible system of incarceration' and make immediate and concrete moves to fix the problem. He's frustrated by circular talk about 'reform,' but there is a deeper, righteous anger here at that species of denial that allows for a population of 2.3 million Americans to be written off as disposable. . . . After reading Moskos's necessary book, it is hard to view such ignorance, such denial, as anything less than ethically repugnant, a violation of our responsibilities as citizens."
—*Rain Taxi Review of Books*

"*In Defense of Flogging* is actually about prisons, and how and why they don't work. Moskos incorporates a brisk and readable history of the development of prisons, and wonders at our addiction to them, notwithstanding our bad results."
—*California Lawyer*

"Moskos's argument is unconventional and convincing. Those interested in prison reform will find much to contemplate here."
—*Library Journal*

"This short, punchy book . . . offers a convincing portrait of the dire situation of American prisons, in which overcrowded inmates live with the constant threat of violence, sexual and otherwise."
—*The Daily*, the first large-scale daily publication intended specifically for the iPad

"Moskos, an assistant professor at John Jay College of Criminal Justice who specializes in police and criminal science, debates with the utmost seriousness the merits of flogging as an alternative to incarceration. . . . Indeed, when Moskos mentions the possibility of electric shock as another option, readers will begin to wonder if the writer is poking outlandish fun and crafting a notion similar to Swift's 1729 classic 'A Modest Proposal,' using satire to call attention to the 'shame' of our inhumane prison system."
—*Publishers Weekly*

"[Moskos is] not mandating the lash, but suggesting that those convicted of a criminal offense be given an option. . . . If we're capable of taking Moskos' idea as a serious option to incarceration, it could have profound consequences for a nation that incarcerates its citizens at a rate that's seven times as high as the other nations of the world. . . . *In Defense of Flogging* forces the reader to confront issues surrounding incarceration that most Americans would prefer not to think about." —*Cleveland Free Press*

"Once you read his [Moskos's] new book, *In Defense of Flogging*, you might find yourself agreeing with him." —*Metro*

"The American prison . . . in the rare moments that it flickers onto the public consciousness, figures as a remote, surreal, but necessary hell to which we consign the wicked. In his popular tract *In Defense of Flogging*, former Baltimore cop Peter Moskos tries to remedy this neglect. . . . Moskos lays it out clearly and amply. . . . There is no real question that (i) Moskos thinks caning better than incarceration and (ii) can't think of anything better than caning. The conclusion is irresistible."
—*Public Discourse: Ethics, Law, and the Common Good*

"Genuinely provocative. . . . he really has succeeded in making me ask whether I can defend my views about prison."
—Claire Berlinski, author of *There is No Alternative*

"Peter Moskos presents us with a true dilemma, the dreadful alternatives of prison or flogging. To make that stark and Swiftian choice, he compels us to rethink our ideas of cruel and humane, barbaric and civilized, progressive and reactionary. It is invariably jarring to overcome a prejudice or abandon a dearly held belief—I try to avoid doing either—but Moskos makes it an intriguing, if unsettling, experience."—Randy Cohen, former writer of *The New York Times Magazine* column "The Ethicist"

IN

DEFENSE

of

FLOGGING

PETER MOSKOS

BASIC BOOKS

A Member of the Perseus Books Group
New York

Copyright © 2011 by Peter Moskos
Hardcover first published in 2011 by Basic Books,
A Member of the Perseus Books Group
Paperback first published in 2013 by Basic Books

All rights reserved. No part of this book may be reproduced in any manner
whatsoever without written permis-sion except in the case of brief
quotations embodied in critical articles and reviews. For information,
address Basic Books, 250 West 57th Street,
15th Floor, New York, NY 10107.

Books published by Basic Books are available at special discounts for bulk
purchases in the United States by corporations, institutions, and other organizations. For more information, please contact the Special Markets Department at the Perseus Books Group, 2300 Chestnut Street, Suite 200,
Philadelphia, PA 19103, or call (800) 810-4145, ext. 5000, or e-mail
special.markets@perseusbooks.com.

Typeset in 12 point Adobe Garamond Pro

The Library of Congress has catalogued the hardcover edition as follows:

Moskos, Peter, 1971–
    In defense of flogging / Peter Moskos.
        p. cm.
    Includes bibliographical references and index.
    ISBN 978-0-465-02148-2 (hbk.)—
    ISBN 978-0-465-02379-0 (e-book) 1. Flagellation. 2. Corporal
punishment. I. Title.

HV8613.M67 2011

364.6'7—dc22

                                                            2010054336

ISBN 978-0465-03241-9 (paperback)

To my father, Charles Moskos,
who always loved a crazy idea

IN

DEFENSE

of

FLOGGING

You're about to get whipped. Mentally more than physically. It's going to hurt—but it's supposed to. Flogging is a series of hard, cracking lashes intended to cause jolting pain. Once the experience is over, you'll never be the same.

I write in defense of flogging, something most people consider too radical for debate, not worthy of intellectual discussion. But please, don't put down this book and move on, upset that I even broached the subject. If that's your temptation, bear with me for just a bit longer. My defense of flogging—whipping, caning, lashing, call it what you will—is meant to be provocative but only because something extreme is needed to shatter the status quo. And that, ultimately, is my goal. There are 2.3 million Americans in prison. That is too many. I want to reduce cruelty, and flogging may be the answer. My opening gambit is simple: Given the choice between five years in prison and ten brutal lashes, which would you choose?

I won't dispute that flogging is a severe and even brutal form of punishment. Under the lash, skin is literally ripped from the body. But very little could be worse than years in prison—removed from society and all you love. Going to prison means losing a part of your life and everything you care for. Compared to this, flogging is just a few very painful strokes on the behind. And it's over in a few minutes. If you had the choice, if you were given the option of staying out of jail, wouldn't you choose to be flogged and released? Think about it: five years hard time or ten lashes on the behind? You'd probably choose flogging. Wouldn't we all?

Having to make this choice isn't as abstract as you may think. After all, who hasn't committed a crime? Perhaps you've taken illegal drugs. Maybe you once got into a fight with a friend, stranger, or lover. Or you drove back from a bar drunk. Or you clicked on an online picture of somebody who turned out to be a bit young. Maybe you're outdoorsy and were caught hunting without a permit.

Or maybe you're a boss who knowingly hired illegal immigrants. Perhaps you accepted a "gift" from a family member and told the IRS it was a loan. Or did you go for the white-collar big leagues and embezzle millions of dollars? In truth, you may be committing some crimes you don't even know about. If your luck runs out, you can end up in jail for almost anything, big or small. And even if you're convinced that you're the most straitlaced, law-abiding person in the world, imagine that through some horrific twist of fate, you were accused of a crime. It's not inconceivable; it happens all the time.

We send thousands of people to jail and prison every day, and each one experiences something similar to this. Imagine you're in court, even though you never expected to be in this position. Maybe things got out of hand and one thing led to another, or maybe you're even innocent. No matter, because now you're standing in court, behind the defense table, looking up to the judge. He (because this isn't a TV show, the judge will probably be a white man) looks at you tiredly, says "guilty," sentences you to five years in prison, says a few more words, and bangs his gavel. You're in shock. Your lawyer shrugs, trying to look sympathetic. But he doesn't seem nearly as bothered as you are. You try to ignore the sobs of your family as a court officer cuffs your hands behind your back.

You're guilty as charged. So whether you did it or not—it strangely doesn't matter anymore—you're officially a criminal. Five years in prison is a long time. Where were you five years ago? Perhaps you've accomplished a lot in the past half-decade. Perhaps you had ambitious plans for the next five years. Whatever your plans were, they're not going to happen now. Before they lead you out the back of the courtroom to a holding room, you seriously ponder many things about prison you've tried hard to avoid. Your lover or spouse may leave you (or at least have an affair). Whatever you're needed for, you're not going to be there. If you have kids, they're going to miss you, and be missed by you. Over the coming years, will your friends visit? And if they don't, what can you do? There's a very good chance that, when you emerge after your time is up, you're going to be alone and unemployed.

Taking away a large portion of somebody's life through incarceration is a strange concept, especially if it's rooted not in actual punishment but rather in some hogwash about making you a better person (more on that later). But what about prison itself? Prison is first and foremost a home of involuntary confinement, a "total institution" of complete dominance and regulation. It's a very strange home indeed that holds 2.3 million people against their will. But what is it like? Will you have to learn prison lingo? Will you be forced to wear funny striped pants and make friends with characters like the Birdman of Alcatraz? No, of course not. That was years ago, and a movie. But what's it like today? Are there drugs, gangs, and long times in solitary? Will you come out stronger—or broken? Will you be raped? Hopefully it's not like the brutal TV show *Oz*? God, you hope not. But you don't know. And that's the rub. Prison is a mystery to all but the millions of people forced to live and work in this gigantic government-run detention system. And as long as we don't look at what happens on the inside, as long as we refuse to consider alternatives, nothing will change.

Is flogging still too cruel to contemplate? If so, given the hypothetical choice between prison and flogging, why did you choose flogging? Perhaps it's not as crazy as you thought. And even if you're adamant that flogging is a barbaric, inhuman form of punishment, how can offering the choice be so bad? If flogging were really worse than prison, nobody would choose it. So what's the harm in offering corporal punishment as an alternative to incarceration? But of course most people would choose to be caned over being sent to prison. And that's my point. Faced with the choice between hard time and the lash, the lash is better. What does that say about prison?

If you think the choice between flogging and prison is a false choice, that there should be a third option, go right ahead and propose it. Perhaps there is another way—neither incarceration nor flogging—that punishes the guilty, provides the convicted with a halfway decent chance of a future, expresses society's disapproval, and satisfies a victim's sense of justice. It's possible, but I doubt it. Do not let eternal optimism damn the future.

Prisons don't work, but unfortunately neither does traditional opposition to them. Without more radical debate, preachers for prison reform will never be heard beyond the choir. There is no shortage of ideas on such things as rehab, job training, indeterminate sentencing, restorative justice, prison survival, and reentry. A search for "prison" books on Amazon.com yields 23,000 results (and almost none are pro-penitentiary). By contrast, a similar search for "flogging" reveals 247 books (and most are about sex). There are many, many books out there about the evils of prison—and to what end? Over the past decades reformers have preached with rational passion and barely controlled anger about the horrors of prison growth; all the while, the government has not so quietly built the largest prison system the world has ever seen.

If we wish to punish criminals, and we do, flogging a man—shaming him and hurting him briefly—is better than the long-term mental torture of incarceration. Over the past two centuries, flogging has gradually disappeared from our criminal code. Although sixty years have passed since the last legal judicial flogging in America, corporal punishment has a long history in American criminal justice.

Many undoubtedly see the demise of flogging as a sign of progress—the end of one more barbarity. Flogging may indeed be barbaric, but maybe barbarism has a bad rap. To the ancient Greeks, after all, barbarians were just foreigners who talked funny: "Bar-bar-bar!" Athenians howled, politically incorrect before their time. Similarly, my defense of flogging may sound barbaric and otherworldly to modern Western ears. But barbaric or not, if we don't discuss flogging, we're stuck with something far worse. In the world of punishment, we're lost; it's time to admit as much and ask directions. For now, let's at least backtrack from this horribly mistaken journey we've taken into the Bizarro World of mass incarceration.

I don't want to add caning to an already brutal system of prison; instead, I propose an alternative to incarceration, what might be called "flog-and-release." Deciding between prison and the lash is truly a choice between the lesser of two evils, but at least it is a choice. No matter what you would choose, if you would want that choice for yourself, why, in the name of compassion and humanity, would you deny that choice to others?

So no, in case you were wondering, this discussion of flogging won't be anything kinky. Outside of an intellectual game, more thought experiment than policy proposal, there's very little pleasure here. My intention is to shock the elite and shake up the debate. My argument is painful and meant to be, but I hope we'll have some fun along the way. And if you're not careful, you may learn something before it's done. Allow me to defend flogging.

• • •

Let's return to your day in court. Before you're led out of the courtroom, the judge calls for order and offers you the flogging option. "Five years or ten lashes," he says. If you choose flogging, an appointed state flogger will cane you immediately. Ten lashes, a little rubbing alcohol, a few bandages, and you'd be free to go home and sleep in your own bed. No holding cell. No lock-up. A quick and painful caning, and you'll be on your way. Would you choose years in the joint over a brief punishment, however cruel? Before you started reading, you probably couldn't imagine wanting to be flogged. But now, I assume, to avoid prison, you've chosen it for yourself. Though it's strange to conceive of being sentenced to a legal flogging, you can probably imagine what it would be like to be caned. Hopefully you've never seen anybody flogged or experienced this personally, but it's not hard to imagine the process.

Consider the case of Aaron Cohen, a New Zealander arrested with his drug-addicted mother for possessing heroin in Malaysia. His mother was sentenced to death and Aaron was sentenced to six lashes plus life in prison. Ultimately, in 1996, five years after Aaron was flogged, his mother's life was spared, and they were both released. In a magazine interview, Aaron described being flogged:

> I got six. It's just incredible pain. More like a burning—like someone sticking an iron on your bum. . . . Afterwards my bum looked like a side of beef. There was three lines of raw skin with blood oozing out. . . . You can't sleep and can only walk like a duck. Your whole backside is three or four times bigger—swollen, black and blue. I made a full recovery within a month and am left with only slight scarring. Emotionally, I'm okay. I haven't had any nightmares about that day, although I'm starting to dream about the prison.

The actual flogging I propose is based on the Singapore and Malaysian models, but it's different in several important ways. Once you consent to be flogged—a luxury you don't have in Singapore or Malaysia—you'd be led into a room where an attending physician would conduct an examination to make sure you're physically fit enough to be flogged, that you won't die under the intense shock of the cane. The punishment would not be a public spectacle but would not be closed to the public. There would be perhaps a dozen spectators, including bailiffs and other representatives of the court, a lawyer, a doctor, perhaps a court reporter, and maybe a few relatives of both parties, including the victim. After the doctor's approval, a guard would tie your arms and legs to a trestle-like whipping post designed specifically for this purpose. This strange piece of furniture resembles a large and sturdy wooden artist's easel, but in place of a painting or canvas, you would be tied somewhat spread-eagle to the front. Once the guard takes down your pants and adds a layer of padding over your back (to protect vital organs from errant strokes), the flogging would begin. An expert trained in the use of the cane would lash your rear end for the prescribed number of times. This flogging description from a Singapore newspaper captures the quick brutality of the procedure:

> When caning, a warder, wielding a half-an-inch-thick and four-feet-long cane, uses the

whole of his body weight, and not just the strength of his arms, to strike. As a result the skin at the point of contact is usually split open and, after three strokes, the buttocks will be covered with blood. All the strokes prescribed by the court . . . are given at one and the same time, at half minute intervals. . . .

The stroke follows the count, and the succeeding count is usually made about half a minute after the stroke has landed. Most of the prisoners put up a violent struggle after each of the first three strokes. Mr. Quek [the prison director] said: "After that, their struggles lessen as they become weaker. At the end of the caning, those who receive more than three strokes will be in a state of shock. Many will collapse, but the medical officer and his team of assistants are on hand to revive them and apply antiseptic on the caning wound."

Your ten strokes would be over in about five minutes. My defense of flogging gives you a minute for every year you would otherwise have served in prison. You'll likely be in shock and perhaps even unconscious as the doctor treats the deep, bloody furrows left in your behind. Then, once they've patched you up, you'd be allowed to leave the courthouse a free man—no striped pajamas, no gangs, no learning from other criminals, no fear. You'd never have to find out what the inside of a prison is like.

If that deal seems too good to be true, well, at least we've moved beyond the facile position that flogging is too painful or cruel to consider. Indeed, if you think that someone subjected to this punishment is getting off too easy—that a man with five years left to serve should not be freed after submitting to *only* ten brutal, skin-bursting, scar-creating lashes—if that's your reaction, then consider this: It would be ironic (actually quite disturbing) if prisons were to remain as they are precisely because of their unparalleled cruelty.

If, however, you think I'm a monster for even hypothetically considering flogging, think of this worse reality: 2.3 million Americans already live behind bars. That's more than 1 percent of our entire adult population. And if that doesn't sound like a lot, let's put this number in perspective. At a sold-out baseball game in Chicago, forty-one thousand people can watch the Cubs at Wrigley

Field. Two-point-three million is more than fifty-six sold-out ballgames. Two-point-three million is roughly the total number of American military personnel—army, navy, air force, marines, coast guard, reserves, and National Guard. Even the army of correctional officers needed to guard 2.3 million prisoners outnumbers the US Marines. If we condensed our nationwide penal system into a single city, it would be the fourth largest city in America, with a population greater than Baltimore, Boston, and San Francisco combined.

America now has more prisoners than any other country in the world. Ever. In sheer numbers and as a percentage of the population. Our rate of incarceration is roughly seven times that of Canada or any Western European country. Stalin, at the height of the Soviet gulag, had fewer prisoners than America does now (although the chances of living through US incarceration are quite a bit higher). Despite our "land of the free" motto, we deem it necessary to incarcerate more of our people than the world's most draconian regimes. Think about it: We have more prisoners than China, and they have *a billion* more people than we do.

It didn't used to be this way. In 1970, before the war on drugs and a plethora of get-tough laws increased sentence lengths and the number of non-violent offenders in prison, we incarcerated 338,000 people. There was even talk of abolishing prison altogether and the hope that prisons would be left on the ash heap of history. But that didn't happen. The prison-abolition movement seems to have died right after a 1973 Presidential Advisory Commission said, "No new institutions for adults should be built, and existing institutions for juveniles should be closed," and concluded, "The prison, the reformatory and the jail have achieved only a shocking level of failure." Since then, even though violent crime in America has gone down, the incarceration rate has increased a whopping 500 percent.

Some have linked this drop in crime to the increase in prisons. To oversimplify a bit, if more muggers are behind bars for longer periods of time, they can't mug you as much. Granted, if everybody were in prison, there would be no crime on the street. But this extreme, appealing though it may be for its logical simplicity, fails for several reasons. Between 1947 and 1991 the prison population increased from 259,000 to 1.2 million. During this time the homicide rate nearly doubled, from 6.1 to 10.5 per hundred thousand. Today the homicide rate is back to where it was in 1947—and yet now we have two million more people behind bars than we did then. Even if prison were responsible for some of the recent crime drop, we're not getting much bang for the buck.

To understand the uselessness of incarceration—to appreciate just how specious the connection between increased incarceration and decreased crime really is—consider New York City. Not only did New York drastically cut crime, it did so while incarcerating fewer people. New York has seen the most significant crime drop of any big city in America: real, substantial, sustained, and, over the past two decades, twice the national average. In 1990 there were 2,245 murders in New York City. In 2010 there were 532. During this period of decreasing crime—and while the city's population increased by more than a million people—the number of incarcerated New Yorkers actually *decreased* by eleven thousand. Less crime should equal fewer prisons. This seems obvious, but it's not the case in the rest of the nation. Had New York followed national patterns and increased its incarceration rate by 65 percent, the city, with an additional fifty-eight thousand prisoners, may very well have bankrupted the state. To incarcerate that many more people from New York City would cost roughly $2 billion per year, nearly doubling the size and cost of the entire state's Department of Corrections.

Better policing and massive immigration—not increased incarceration—contributed to New York's crime drop. In the 1990s the NYPD got back in the crime *prevention* game: Drug dealers were pushed indoors, and crack receded in general. Also, police focused on quality-of-life issues, the so-called "broken windows." At the same time more than one million foreign immigrants moved to New York City. Whether due to a strong work ethic, fear of deportation, traditional family values, or having the desire and means to emigrate in the first place, immigrants (nationwide and in New York City) have lower rates of crime and incarceration than native-born Americans. Astoundingly, today more than one in three New Yorkers are foreign born. Although policing in New York City deservedly received a lot of credit for the city's crime drop, strangely, few people credit immigrants and almost nobody seemed to notice the winning strategy of "decarceration."

Looking elsewhere in the United States, we can see even more refutations of the connection between imprisonment and crime rates. Crime rates have spiked and fallen quite independent of prison rates, which have only gone up. If we were to give increased incarceration credit for the crime drop of the past two decades, we could just as easily give it credit for the crime increase in the two decades before that. From 1970 to 1991 crime rose while we locked up a million more people. Since then we've locked up another million and crime has gone down. So what's so special about that *second* million? Were they the only ones who were "real criminals"? Did we simply get it wrong with the first 1.3 million people we put behind bars? Because the incarceration rate has only gone up since 1970, we could correlate anything with this increase. We could just as easily credit incarceration with the collapse of Communism or the Boston Red Sox winning the World Series.

One reason prison doesn't reduce crime is that many prison-worthy offenses—especially drug crimes—are economically demand-motivated. This doesn't change when a drug dealer is locked up. Contrast that with, say, pedophilia: An active pedophile taken off the streets means fewer raped children. A child victim doesn't go out searching for another criminal abuser. But that's exactly what a drug addict does.

An arrest in the war on drugs usually creates a job opening. Arrest thousands of drugs dealers (and pay millions of dollars for their incarceration), and other needy or greedy people will take their place. Nothing else will change. As long as dealing drugs is profitable, which it can be, there will be a never-ending supply of arrestable and imprisonable offenders. The war on drugs may have started as a response to a drug problem, but it's created an even larger and entirely preventable *prohibition* problem.

Prison reformers—and I wish them well—tinker at the edges of a massive failed system. I'm all for what are called "intermediate sanctions": House monitoring, GPS bracelets, intensive parole supervision, fines, restitution, drug courts, and day-reporting centers all show promise and deserve our full support. But we need much more drastic action. To bring our incarceration back to a civilized level—one we used to have and much more befitting a rich, modern nation—we would have to reduce the number of prisoners by 85 percent. Without alternative punishments, this will not happen anytime soon. Even the most optimistically progressive opponent of prison has no plan to release two million prisoners.

There might be other ways to reduce the prison population, but none of these seem particularly viable. We could legalize and regulate drugs and also get soft on crime, but that's also not likely to happen anytime soon. And we can't and shouldn't just swing open the prison gates and shout, "Olly olly oxen free!" We need to maintain some balance of justice, punishment, and public safety.

As ugly as it may seem, corporal punishment would be an effective and, believe it or not, comparatively humane way to bring our prison population back in line with world standards. To those in prison we could offer the lash in exchange for sentence years, after the approval of some parole board designed to keep the truly dangerous behind bars. As a result, our prison population would plummet. This would not only save money but save prisons for those who truly deserve to be there: the uncontrollably dangerous. Let us not confuse a need to incapacitate—because someone *will* commit a crime—with the concept of punishment—because someone *has* committed a crime.

Certainly mere drug offenders should not be kept in prison, nor should white-collar criminals. Bernard Madoff, famously convicted in 2009 for running a massive Ponzi scheme, is being incarcerated and costing the public even more money. Why? He's no threat to society. Nobody would give him a penny to invest. But Madoff did wrong and deserves to be punished. Better to cane him and let him go. Punishment is, after all, a vital goal of the criminal justice system. Even if the successful rehabilitation of criminals were always possible, it wouldn't be enough. When people commit a crime, they should be punished.

To understand how important punishment is to the notion of justice, imagine being the victim of a violent mugging. The last thing you remember before slipping into unconsciousness is the mugger pissing on you and laughing. Such things happen. Luckily, police catch the bastard, and he is quickly convicted. What should happen next?

What if there were some way to reform this violent criminal *without punishing him*? In *Sleeper*,

Woody Allen's futuristic movie from the 1970s, there's a device like a small walk-in closet called the "orgasmatron." A person goes in and closes the door, lights flash, and three seconds later, well . . . that's why they call it the orgasmatron. Now imagine, if you will, a device similar to the orgasmatron called the "reformatron." It's the perfect rehabilitation machine for criminals. Upon conviction, felons enter this box and close the door. Three seconds later they come out slightly disheveled and "cured" of all their criminal tendencies. Your mugger, therefore, would be ushered into the reformatron, which is conveniently located right in the courtroom. In he goes: The door closes, the lights flash, and three seconds later . . . success! The cured criminal thanks God, kisses his baby's mother, and walks out of the courtroom a free man to go home, relax, and think about job possibilities.

For many reformers in the criminal justice system, the reformatron is the ideal. But along with being fiction, the concept is disturbingly lacking in justice. If you were the victim of a violent mugging—if you had been beaten, pissed on, and robbed of your money, health, and dignity—would the reformatron satisfy your sense of justice? The fact that the criminal wouldn't commit another crime is nice, but shouldn't a criminal be punished—not only for his sake but also for ours?

Retributive justice is part of every society and deeply rooted in American culture. Consider the death penalty, which has always had strong public support in America. There is almost no evidence, despite what many Americans want to believe, that the death penalty deters crime. Yet even among those who know the death penalty does not deter crime, support for the death penalty still runs three to one. Deterrence and punishment are separate issues. Punishment is about retribution. Reformers have a tough time grasping this.

The problem—and our shame—is that prisons, though never designed for this purpose, have become the only way we punish. In an ironic twist, we designed the prison system to replace flogging. The penitentiary was supposed to be a kinder and gentler sentence, one geared to personal salvation, less crime, and a better life for all. It was, in short, intended to serve the function of a reformatron. Needless to say, it didn't work.

Before we had prisons, those who violated laws were generally subject to pain, exile, shame, or death. Whipping, fines, and the stocks were common criminal punishments in British colonies. Though people could receive the death penalty for many minor crimes, including such vague offenses as "malicious mischief," people, or at least the intellectual elite, considered flogging barbaric and primitive. Despite the harshness of the justice system, none of these punishments seemed to work: They didn't deter crime.

It isn't difficult to imagine the history of our present prison system—throwing criminals into cages for substantial portions of their adult lives—as a process of steady evolution away from corporal punishment. Perhaps first one person was kept in a cage instead of being flogged or put in the stockades, and then another person was thrown in too. But perhaps the cage was kind of small, so the guards built another cage. And then the authorities would have built big walls and more cages. One could imagine this transition toward the modern prison, but that's not how it happened.

Before we had prisons, harsh confinement was used alongside corporal punishment. But such incarceration generally had another purpose, such as holding a person until trial, or until a debt was paid. Confinement was a means to an end: People weren't sentenced to confinement; they were held until something else could happen. And jails of the day were different—often communal affairs in which men and women mingled, sometimes with the lubrication of free-flowing liquor. Friends and family could visit, too, and often needed to because they might be the sole providers of a prisoner's necessities, food included. Jail wasn't meant to be long-term or especially sustainable, so inmates without money or friends could—and sometimes did—die from illness or the elements.

Political prisoners and prisoners of war were often locked up to keep them out of commission. This is similar in practice to a modern prison, but generally the actual numbers involved were quite small. One exception, however, was during the American Revolution. One historian estimates that some 17,500 American soldiers and sailors—more than double the number killed in actual battle—died of disease and starvation aboard British prison ships docked in New York City.

Even our own George Washington sent a few prisoners to a horribly bizarre jail. Months after taking control of the Continental Army, the general and future president packed off a few "flagrant and atrocious villains" to a Connecticut dungeon fashioned from an abandoned copper mine. The convicts arrived with a letter from Washington stating rather tersely that the men had been tried and found guilty by a court martial (the letter did not specify the actual crime). General Washington informed the jail keepers that they would "be pleased" to secure the prisoners in their jail or anywhere else "so that they cannot possibly make their escape." As for payment, Washington asked for credit. In these cases there was no pretense of punishment (which could easily have been meted out in other manners) nor any desire to "cure" the criminal; prisoners were simply left to rot.

Given the gruesome history of confinement, in the late 1700s the concept of a penitentiary was truly radical and cutting-edge. The study of criminals was a growing academic field, one that reflected new notions about medicine and science emerging at the time. People believed, somewhat naively, that no healthy man would choose a life of crime. And if new medicines could cure physical ailments, well then why not cure criminal ailments as well? Just as doctors in hospitals were healing the physically sick, could not trained prison professionals cure criminal illness? And just as today we would never consider beating Satan out of a schizophrenic, reformers of that era hoped that corporal punishment—indeed punishment of any sort—would soon be seen as similarly outdated. And even if reformers could not completely cure criminals, perhaps they could heal at least certain "degenerate" criminal types (at the time generally associated with blacks and swarthy immigrants) just enough to function in proper society.

Today we know that prisons are not hospitals for the criminally ill (though prisons do house many mentally ill people, to horrible effect). At the time, however, many people hoped that we could purge criminality from a person's system. The mantra of reformers became "treat not the crime, but the criminal." Alas, crime is often an act of free will, and it happens most when people are angry, drunk, jealous, in need of money or a high, or just in the wrong place at the wrong time. Human nature is not a virus or a genetic illness to be cured, and thinking of crime in terms of degenerate biological types has led to some of the worst horrors humankind has seen.

• • •

Cesare Beccaria, an Italian politician and philosopher, came up with the idea of deterrence in his 1764 *Essay on Crimes and Punishments*. Beccaria transformed theories of criminality. Contrary to popular beliefs, Beccaria posited that the Devil himself did not actually possess criminals. Instead, said Beccaria, people have free will to act rationally to serve their own self-interests. When crime paid less, he suggested, there would be fewer criminals. So in order to deter potential offenders, punishment must be swift, certain, and proportional to the crime.

Despite the difficulties of putting Beccaria's theories into practice, these notions of deterrence and crime prevention form the basis of what is now known as the classical school of criminology. Beccaria's revolutionary ideas crossed the ocean to a receptive America. Over the past two centuries his concepts have worked their way into the very core of American justice and punishment. Reformers wanted to create a modern system of justice appropriate for a newly independent and enlightened republic. In America the British system of execution and harsh flogging gave way to what was supposed to be a softer and reforming system of penitentiaries. Solitary confinement replaced the lash, and prison replaced public shaming. At the time, this all seemed like progress.

As a founding father of criminology, Beccaria helped lay the cornerstone for the modern American justice system—but maybe he was wrong. Classic deterrence theory, like the more modern cost-benefit analysis, depends on a certain level of rational thought and long-term comprehension that seems to be lacking in criminals who are desperate, high, or mentally disturbed. There's little evidence that most criminals consider possible punishment before committing a crime. They don't think they'll be caught. Academics continue to debate the root causes of crime, but crime prevention may rest less in grand sociological and economic theories than in effective policing and more informal social control.

Although Beccaria came up with the groundbreaking notion that something could serve as a deterrent to potential criminals, the idea of putting people into cells, supposedly for their own good, gets credited to John Howard, a well-off Calvinist born in 1726. Howard believed that isolation was the way to moral and physical salvation and knew firsthand how criminal knowledge and physical diseases spread in the filthy communal atmosphere of jail. In 1755 French privateers captured the ship Howard was on, and he was briefly imprisoned. Back home, in 1773, Howard was a county sheriff and found the conditions of the local jail appalling. He then visited hundreds of other jails and documented all of this in his extremely influential book, *The State of the Prisons in England and Wales*. Solitary confinement, he believed, provided an environment much more conducive to salvation and healing.

Based on Howard's vision, a small jail in Wymondham, England, was rebuilt in 1787 on the principles of hard labor, solitary confinement, and penance (hence the name "penitentiary"). Men and women were no longer allowed to mingle, and all prisoners were separated into individual cells where they ate, slept, and worked alone (inmate labor was supposed to pay for the prison's upkeep, but it almost never does—forced labor is rarely good labor). The idea was for prisoners to remain in their monk-like cells until, hallelujah, they were cured of their criminal ways. The miraculously religious imperative behind Howard's system was shaky at best, and yet this little town jail became the basis for the penitentiary system in America and then the world.

In the United States, Quaker reformers in Pennsylvania were the first to take up the penitentiary cause. The fact that Quakers are responsible for creating prisons may seem odd, but consider the potential appeal of solitary confinement to a denomination that formed in opposition to Calvinists' belief in predestination, preached salvation through personal experience of the divine, and worshipped in silence. Rather than punishing criminals' bodies, Quakers, like many other prison reformers, wanted to save their souls.

So in 1787 the Philadelphia Society for Alleviating the Miseries of Public Prisons was established by Quaker-raised Benjamin Rush. The Society condemned the jails and public punishments of its time, proposing that isolating prisoners in solitary cells would be more effective than flogging. The key to this belief is a firm and paternalistic conviction that crime is a moral disease. Particularly galling to reformers like Rush was the loose atmosphere of the era's jails, with their alcohol and race-blind mixing of men and women. Although Rush, a signatory of the Declaration of Independence, was perhaps America's most respected doctor, the science he practiced was quite primitive. The good doctor, for instance, prescribed mercury as a curative, lanced patients to bleed them of bile, and believed that African Americans suffered from the possibly curable hereditary disease of "negroidism." As they say, a little knowledge can be a dangerous thing. And Rush's attitudes toward criminals were equally wrong.

For reformers like Rush, the penitentiary ideas of John Howard and utilitarian philosophy of Jeremy Bentham offered a modern and scientific alternative to contemporaneous jails. Bentham's *Panopticon*, written the same year Rush established the Prison Society, offered "a new mode of obtaining power of mind over mind, in a quantity hitherto without example . . . all by a simple idea in Architecture!" Today this sounds simultaneously naive and sinister, but Bentham's *Panopticon* and "hedonic calculus"—people do what gives them the greatest pleasure—hugely influenced prison design and philosophy. The essential characteristic of the Panopticon is total physical and psychological surveillance and control though a combination of isolation, monitoring, and "apparent omnipresence." In practice, this meant a single, centrally located dark guard booth (dark so it could see but not be seen) with a direct line of sight to a stacked circle of surrounding cells.

Pennsylvania overhauled its criminal code in 1790 based on the recommendations of Rush and his Society. The commonwealth abolished flogging and commissioned the establishment of America's first "penitentiary." It got off to a rocky start. To begin with, the location, a newly built annex of Philadelphia's Walnut Street Jail, was problematic. Walnut Street Jail already had a boss, one John Reynolds—and he had been there for ten years. Reynolds wrote nothing for posterity, so we know of him mostly through his enemies, who called him "uncouth" and scorned him as an "unsympathetic hireling of the county sheriff . . . in no way disposed to permit the ministers to enter the prison to preach their sermon." But the fact that Reynolds, a former tavern owner, had little desire to humor teetotaling, Bible-thumping preachers and their newfangled theories of criminality is not entirely surprising. As jailer, Reynolds was not paid, so he earned a living as best he could. Said his opponents: "One reason why all the prisoners, without discrimination, are admitted into the hall together is that liquor is sold at the door by small measure, by the gaoler." Well, of course it was. Alcohol was a major part of civic life, and teetotaling made little sense—especially not in jail, and surely not if you sold the booze.

Reynolds may have been unpopular with Philadelphia prison reformers, but he was not without friends in high places. Starting in 1785, five years before Pennsylvania's great criminal justice reforms, Reynolds's boss was General Thomas Procter of Revolutionary War fame. Procter, in turn, just happened to be a friend and drinking buddy of President George Washington. Presumably this made Procter no friend of Benjamin Rush, who was long Washington's political adversary.

Still, though it took five years, Rush's reformers eventually won. In 1795 Reynolds left the jail, and Walnut Street Jail transformed into the Walnut Street Penitentiary. The prisoners, naturally, were terrified of the reformers' vision. On the evening of the first day of the "grand experiment," the prisoners voted with their feet in a mass jailbreak; 15

of them succeeded. After that, however, things set-
tled into a grim normalcy. Between 45 and 145
prisoners entered Walnut Street annually, but actual
solitary confinement facilities were available for only
a third of those admitted. The rest "lie on the floor,
on a blanket, and about thirty sleep in one room;
they are strictly prohibited from keeping their
clothes on at night"—and that from a sympathetic
account. The new penitentiary prohibited alcohol
and segregated prisoners by race, sex, and type of
crime. Furthermore, "hardened criminals" were kept
from first-time offenders. Many of these basic concepts of categorization are still with us—even racial
segregation. California prisons, for instance, openly
practiced racial segregation until 2005 and still
haven't resolved issues of racially based gangs.

Looking back at some of these prison reformers'
writings, it's striking how they could be so knowingly cruel and even sadistic despite their supposedly
good intentions. In an 1811 account, one doctor
proudly noted that the guards at Walnut Street carried "no weapons, not even a stick." Fine, but instead
of whipping prisoners, the prison guards withheld
food to maintain order. Because families could
no longer visit and provide for their locked-up

loved ones, the prison officials had total control over the inmates:

> The solitary cells and low diet have on all occasions been found amply sufficient to bring down the most determined spirit, to tame the most hardened villain that ever entered them. Of the truth of this there are striking cases on record. Some veterans in vice, with whom it was necessary to be severe, have declared their preference of death by the gallows, to a further continuance in that place of torment. In the cells, the construction of which renders conversation among those confined in them difficult, the miserable man is left to the greatest of all possible punishments, his own reflections. His food, which consists of only half a pound of bread per day, is given him in the morning; in the course of a few days or weeks the very nature of the being is changed.

With a half loaf of bread a day for weeks, this "humane" replacement to flogging literally starved men into submission. At this point, the ideals of reformation already seem lost.

As Philadelphia experimented with this new method of containment, New York was not far behind. Crime, as usual, was seen as a growing problem. One early New Yorker recounted a time when "no man would venture beyond Broadway towards the North [Hudson] River by night without carrying pistols, and the watchmen marched on their beats in couples; one to take care of the other." So in 1797, well after the failures of Walnut Street should have been known, New York reformed its criminal code and appointed Thomas Eddy as the warden of the state's first prison, Newgate Prison in Greenwich Village. Eddy, another Philadelphia-born Quaker, was New York's leading prison advocate at the time and slandered corporal punishment as a relic of "barbarous" British imperialism ill suited to "a new country, simple manners, and a popular form of government."

Newgate's approach to solitary confinement, though still allegedly for the prisoner's own benefit, was also clearly punishment. Politically, then as now, prisons started to gather support both from conservative hard-liners who demanded ever more severe sanctions and liberals who desired an alternative to punishment and desperately wanted to believe reformers' curative promises. Eddy offered religious and moral instruction in Newgate, and prisoners who behaved earned special privileges. Those who acted up were thrown into solitary confinement, where, according to Eddy, they could "perceive the wickedness and folly" and experience "the bitter pangs of remorse."

Newgate was overcrowded, dirty, and violent from the get-go. One lawyer for the Society for the Prevention of Pauperism observed that such confinement helped criminals "increase, diffuse, and extend the love of vice, and a knowledge of the arts and practices of criminality." Some noted, as was perfectly obvious, that this new and supposedly curative system of incarceration was driving people insane. After at least four known riots in the first seven years, the city went so far as to organize armed watchmen to surround the prison at night to prevent prisoners from escaping. Then, after yet another serious riot, public disapproval finally forced Eddy out in 1804, seven years after Newgate's opening.

In truth, what happened at Newgate wasn't unique; all prisons have failed. Newgate was just one of the first. But as happened in Pennsylvania in 1790 and New York in 1797, the establishment of a penitentiary system usually went hand in hand with the abolition of corporal punishment. So despite—or perhaps because of—Newgate's failures, New York authorized similar prisons but on a much larger scale. After all, with flogging banned, what was the alternative? New York built upstate Auburn Prison in 1816 and then upriver Sing Sing in 1826. After these new prisons opened, the state sold Newgate to the city of New York, which tore it down in 1828.

What was notable about this second wave of construction (which also included Philadelphia's 1829 Eastern State Penitentiary) was the prisons' stone walls, the multifloored cell blocks, and the massive size we've come to associate with a place that looks like a prison. With these penitentiaries designed for hundreds rather than dozens of prisoners, the modern scale of mass incarceration, an American invention, began.

The public was fascinated with these new institutions and their two competing systems, both of which promoted silence and promised to deliver America from the evils of punishment. New York's Auburn went with a "congregate model" that let prisoners gather in groups for meals and work;

Philadelphia's Eastern State, based on Bentham's solitary ideals (though it lacked the Panopticon's basic circular structure) enforced extreme solitary confinement. To maintain silence, guards wore slippers to muffle footsteps, and tracks carried food carts with leather-covered wheels. When not in the cells (coming or leaving prison, for instance), inmates' heads were covered in hoods. The goal, prison commissioners said, was to keep prisoners so isolated that if they were in prison on election night, they wouldn't know who was president of the United States when they were released. Eastern State even followed Bentham's advice on the delicate subject of "carrying off the result of necessary evacuations." He was not talking about fire drills. Because a common "necessary" room would be dangerous to security and incompatible with solitude, Bentham reluctantly advocated, despite the cost, "having in each cell a fixed provision made for this purpose." Eastern State installed individual flush toilets before even the White House had indoor plumbing.

Then, in 1831 Alexis de Tocqueville came to the United States with his friend Gustave de Beaumont. We sometimes forget that the purpose of what became de Tocqueville's famous *Democracy in*

America was America's new penitentiary system; everything else was lagniappe. The two Frenchmen toured prisons and penitentiaries in this young and still exotic nation. But it is as if Beaumont and de Tocqueville were unwilling to criticize their hosts. They express fondness for nearly everything prison-related except prisoner idleness and one New Orleans jail they describe as "a horrid sink, in which they are thronged together, and which is fit only for those dirty animals found here together with the prisoners."

Their strangely fawning take on Auburn and Eastern State Prison is curious in its contradictions. They somewhat nonsensically claim that Philadelphia's Eastern State "produces more honest men" while Auburn "more obedient citizens." In Auburn Prison, "where they are whipped, they die less frequently than in Philadelphia, where, for humanity's sake, they are put in a solitary and sombre cell." This didn't seem to bother them. Nor did the fact that despite Philadelphia's supposed noncorporal "humanity," prisoners there were "much more unhappy." In the end they pick Philadelphia's Eastern State as best but quickly note that Auburn is "next preferable."

Without doubt Beaumont and de Tocqueville were well aware of the horrible effect of idle solitary confinement. They called such punishment "beyond the strength of man; it destroys the criminal without intermission and without pity; it kills." And yet they remained optimistic about solitary's future application: "Can there be a combination more powerful for reformation than . . . solitude, [which] makes him find a charm in the converse of pious men, whom otherwise he would have seen with indifference, and heard without pleasure?" When they came across an isolated prisoner in Philadelphia who considered a cricket his companion, Beaumont and de Tocqueville waxed lyrically about how ripe his mind must be for "the influence of wise advice and pious exhortation."

Their attitude toward corporal punishment is no less confusing. They claim to oppose the lash, but then make apologies for its use. They insist prisoners in Auburn aren't really whipped that much, that the lash is only "resorted to in extreme cases or not at all." And in Sing Sing, where whippings were more common, Beaumont and de Tocqueville deem it a necessary deterrent, a physical aid to the "moral power" of silence and labor.

After *Democracy in America* was published in 1835, prisons became part of the tourist circuit for travelers of a certain social station. Charles Dickens retraced some of the Frenchmen's steps in 1842 and saw much of the same, such as a prisoner pacing his cell with "both hands clasped on his uplifted head, hear[ing] spirits tempting him to beat his brains out on the wall." But rather than see potential for "pious exhortation," Dickens was justly horrified by this. "In its intention," Dickens says of the penitentiary, "I am well convinced that it is kind, humane, and meant for reformation; but . . . those benevolent gentlemen who carry it into execution, do not know what it is that they are doing. . . . I hold this slow and daily tampering with the mysteries of the brain, to be immeasurably worse than any torture of the body." Dickens concludes that "no man" has the right to inflict such "torture and agony . . . upon his fellow-creature." Dickens wrote, in essence, the precursor to *In Defense of Flogging*.

In the long run the differences between Philadelphia and New York mattered less than de Tocqueville or anybody else imagined. In the nineteenth century, and mostly because of cost, solitary confinement fell out of fashion. Eastern State's hoods, slippers, and silence passed into history. Auburn prison's so-called "congregate system" became the norm not because it was better (though it probably was) but because it was cheaper. Although the congregate system eliminated the worst of the Dickensian horrors, it had significant problems of its own, especially after labor unions, at least in the North, protested with increasing success against convict labor. So prisons, despite their noble aspirations, became little more than human warehouses and boarding schools for criminals.

The congregate prison system was virtually enshrined in 1890 when the Supreme Court declared solitary confinement to be an extreme form of punishment different from standard incarceration, all but banning the practice. The case concerned James Medley, who received a death sentence in Colorado for killing his wife. Between Medley's conviction and execution Colorado passed a law mandating solitary confinement for prisoners on death row. After prison authorities moved Medley to solitary, the court ordered Medley, a convicted killer, freed. In its rationale the court detailed solitary to be "additional punishment of the most important and painful character" and not just "a mere unimportant regulation as to safe-keeping of the prisoner." This made Medley's solitary confinement ex post facto and thus unconstitutional.

For most of the 1900s the court's ruling stuck, and prolonged isolation in solitary confinement was rare. Prisoners were kept in cells (today communal rooming with bunk beds is more common) but allowed freedom of movement and human interaction in cell blocks and recreation yards. Things changed, however, in 1983, when inmates in Marion Prison killed two guards in two separate incidents on the same day. Marion immediately went on lockdown and remained there—for the next twenty-three years. In the process, Marion became the nation's first "supermax" prison.

Supermax prisons are entirely solitary, evoking in function—though decidedly not in spirit—the operation of the original penitentiaries. Reincarnated after nearly a century's absence, the concept of near-total isolation spread from Marion, Illinois, to the world. In supermax, prisoners are fed in their cell, allowed solitary showers a few times a week, and given one hour of "rec time," which is alone, in a caged-in area open to the sky. Disturbingly, nobody knows just how many American prisoners are in solitary confinement. But along with roughly twenty-five thousand supermax prisoners, there are perhaps fifty to eighty thousand more prisoners in maximum security prisons kept in supermax-like isolation in "special housing units" (known as SHU and pronounced like "shoe").

Though the Supreme Court never explicitly overturned *Medley*, a 1989 decision, *Mistretta v. United States*, upheld a sentencing commission that explicitly rejected imprisonment as a means of promoting rehabilitation. This allowed prisons to hold people without any pretense of betterment, thus giving the green light to long-term nonrehabilitative solitary confinement. Despite the court's 1890 warning in *Medley*, getting sent to the SHU is now mostly for punishment or protection—sometimes for guards and other times for prisoners. Although some prisoners may enjoy a few days in isolation as a respite from the horrors of overcrowded communal living, long-term solitary confinement—it's not clear how much time it takes—is a sure way to cause deep psychological damage. A California inmate described the insanity in solitary confinement:

Rarely in a lifetime do we ever witness a sane person go insane. And even more rare is it to witness such an occurrence happen more than once. . . . I thought that seeing a prisoner get shot by staff was a frightening and chilling event, but that in no way compares to seeing a prisoner calmly playing a game of chess with pieces made out of his own feces. Or, prisoners smearing their bodies and cells with their feces. Or, watching prisoners throwing urine and feces at each other through the perforated cell doors. And worse yet . . . we eat our meals under these conditions.

In response to this gulag, this inmate organized—which is no easy task in solitary confinement—a hunger strike of nine hundred prisoners. The strike was specifically to protest a policy that isolated inmates for indefinite periods when they were labeled, often anonymously and sometimes erroneously, as gang members. "The only way for a validated gang member to be released from a SHU," wrote one journalist, "was to be paroled, die, go insane or become an informant on other prisoners." Without even the lip service of rehabilitation—the more modern term for the eighteenth-century notion of "curing" criminality—long-term indefinite isolation has become the ultimate punishment.

Ironically, a professor dedicated to crime prevention and prison reform unwittingly helped destroy the rehabilitative ideal. Robert Martinson was so dedicated to social justice that, as a graduate student in 1961, he was a Freedom Rider jailed in Mississippi as part of a "jail-in," a novel idea to deliberately fill the state's jails. Martinson's national fame came later, with a multiauthored, 735-page tome rather academically titled *The Effectiveness of Correctional Treatment: A Survey of Treatment Evaluation Studies*. The authors, in what is now known as a meta-analysis, looked at existing research and concluded that, statistically speaking, nothing was a proven success. They issued that most academic of clichés: a call for further study. But Martinson, known for his fondness for the media, wasn't done. His 1974 *Public Interest* article on the subject, "What Works?," became known in policy circles as "Nothing Works!" With that moniker, the press misinterpreted Martinson and academics viciously attacked him.

Martinson never believed "nothing works," but he knew damn well that *prisons* do not work. Like many reformers, Martinson just wanted *effective* rehabilitation. But unlike many reformers, Martinson was brutally honest about existing failures. "The press," he later conceded, "has no time for scientific quibbling and got to the heart of the matter better than I did." As such, "nothing works" became the very successful battle cry for the political opposition eager to lock up more people and warehouse them. In the end, the City College of New York denied tenure to the coauthor of what has been called "the most politically important criminological study of the past half century," and, though presumably there were other contributing factors, Martinson killed himself by jumping out a Manhattan window.

. . .

Throughout human history, people have devised truly ingenious and absolutely horrifying ways to punish. Today it's nearly impossible to think of a never-tried form of torture: Amputation, boiling, branding, burning, crucifixion, drowning, freezing, impaling, quartering alive, squeezing, stretching, and suffocating are just starters. In Thailand, for instance, criminals once were squeezed inside a wicker ball, known as the elephant ball, which had nails pointing inward. Then—and here's where they get points for inventiveness—elephants would kick the ball-encased person down a field. But even societies that gleefully hurt others rarely if ever placed a human being in a cell for punishment. Consequently, that we accept prisons as normal is a historical oddity. But it's doubtful that rulers who skinned people alive would think a prison cell was too harsh; it's more likely they just thought it made no sense to pay good money to confine a person in a cell, especially when various forms of corporal punishment were faster and cheaper.

Although the harshness of our modern prison system may not bother the inventor of the elephant ball, the sadism inherent in long-term imprisonment, especially solitary confinement, should give pause to all who have the slightest bit of human empathy. Is anything worse than being entombed alive? Edgar Allan Poe may as well have been commenting on the morality of the prison system when he wrote, "To be buried while alive is, beyond question, the most terrific of these extremes which has ever fallen to the lot of mere mortality." From this, seeing life in prison as the burial of the human soul is but a small metaphorical step. At the same time that Poe was writing, an early Sing Sing warden told inmates, "You are to be literally buried from the world." Charles Dickens called the prison cell a "stone coffin."

Prison is an insidious marriage of entombment and torture. Not only are inmates immured in prison, they are also subjected to never-ending physical and mental agony. Consider one California inmate's account of prison life:

> I live in a bathroom with another man, rarely see my loved ones, I'm surrounded by killers and thieves. . . .
>
> There's no one you can really talk to in here, no one you can trust to not take advantage of a perceived weakness at least. It's hard to be on point all the time, wear your mask and check your armor for cracks. I've been doing this level four, max security shit for over five years now, but haven't been home, haven't been able to hold my daughter, haven't been able to just *be*, for about eight years now.

The conditions in overcrowded modern prisons can be, in the starkest terms, as hellish as their early American prototypes. Bunk beds stacked within arm's reach of each other fill cells and communal sleeping rooms. Although guards may act like they're in charge, because of the sheer numbers, prisons are, in effect, run by prisoners. And without legal forms of settling disputes and conducting transactions, violence and criminality become the norm. One prisoner succinctly summed up the prisoner-survival attitude: "If I gotta survive in this environment, I gotta be bad ass."

The risks of physical and sexual violence in prison, though sometimes overstated, are real enough: Approximately one in twenty prison inmates say they've been sexually assaulted by other inmates or staff in the past year. Because there's no permitted sexual outlet (even masturbation is against the rules), there's a lot of sexual aggression. And yet we still joke about prison rape. An online article, presumably written by a correctional officer, describes the realities of prison rape:

> Although it can occur, it is not as prevalent as it was in past years. Technology, increased staff

members, and better construction tactics have improved surveillance over the years.

When an inmate is forcibly raped by a group of men, usually another uninvolved inmate will offer the raped inmate protection from gang rapes, but it carries a price. The inmate must now have sex with the protector. As bad as this sounds, it is better than being raped. The inmate has the option of "checking off," that is asking prison staff for protection. This too carries a price. Prison officials often ask the inmate to identify, and testify against his attackers. At this point, the inmate is labeled a "snitch," and his life is in further danger.

In what is perhaps the most graphic depiction of prison sex to reach the American public, comedian Chris Rock popularized an account of life behind bars that was so over the top it became known as the "Tossed Salad Man." The original (decidedly noncomedic) version appeared in an HBO documentary in which one large and charismatic gay prisoner described his modus operandi in all-too-clear terms: "First of all, if he's a newcomer, I want him to suck my ass with jelly. That's the slang word, tossing salad. It means sucking my ass, right? With jelly or without jelly. Some people prefer syrup. I prefer the guy to use jelly." According to the prisoner, the nominally straight man can at least pretend he's licking a woman. The prisoner then attempts to re-assure the viewer: "It's clean. The person is decent." Chris Rock declared the Tossed Salad Man a greater deterrent to crime than the death penalty. And yet although most of us would never wish this sort of experience on another human being, by allowing the prison system to continue unchecked, we effectively do just that.

Without gang protection or a long-term com-mittment to solitary confinement, the danger of sex-ual assault is ever-present. Take this account from another inmate:

> My biggest fear of being in this place isn't, you know, getting out alive is something, too, but you don't have to do anything to become a vic-tim. And there's no one man strong enough to come against a group of five or six. And if some-body gets a wild idea in their mind, that they want to do something obscene or what have it

to you, there's nothing I can do if they catch
me in the wrong spot and the wrong time.

Faced with this predicament, some prisoners submit
to semiconsensual sexual acts. Still others simply
make do with whatever options are available.

The perpetual threat of violence, sexual or
otherwise, is interspersed with long periods of monotony. This account comes from an online prisoner
message board:

> At the end of the day it's the fucking boredom.
> I'm surprised prisons aren't worse than what
> they are. You ever see what happens when you
> just give nothing to do to high schoolers or
> middle schoolers? It won't last long, they'll come
> up with something to do which will likely hurt
> someone or break something. Now imagine if
> those kids are grown men there for violent of-
> fenses. Now imagine if there was some kind of
> society built around this concept. BAM! Prison.

In response to boredom and fear, many prisoners
turn to drugs and alcohol to pass the time. Drugs,

smuggled in by guards and visitors alike, are readily available in prison (the inability to keep even prisons free of drugs is perhaps the best illustration of the futility of the war on drugs). One prison dealer estimated that 75 percent of prisoners get high. He put it this way:

> If it wasn't for drugs in this prison, you'd have a lotta more violence going around. Ain't nothin' in here. Ain't *nothing* in here. So when you got anger and frustration and prison and time, that's going to breed violence. So now when you got a little something that is going to sedate the violence? They should be lucky guys like me is inside the penitentiary.

If you're stuck in prison, why *wouldn't* you take drugs? What else are you going to do?

Prisoners seek out the standard recreational drugs, particularly marijuana, alcohol, and heroin, as well as legal prescribed pharmaceuticals, which have the added benefit of being free when administered by medical staff. In prison, drugs get marked up anywhere from five to forty times their street value, with the price generally rising with increased distance from a big city. Payment happens in cash (which is also illegally smuggled into prisons), commissary accounts, and any material possession, as well as through nonincarcerated friends. "I mean," says one drug dealer, "how would you pay if you owed me money and you were in prison, and you were scared for your life? You'd pay the best way you knew how. You would call your people: 'Get me some money down here.' You'd find family from somewhere to get you some money down here." But if you can't pay? "You'd become my"—this is how the drug dealer puts it—"something like a jail slave. Every time you get paid, it would go to me. Until I feel as though the debt is paid." Compared to this, flogging looks better and better. Undoubtedly flogging is no dream, but at least it won't put you in deeper debt.

To outsiders, prison is a black box, a mystery of hellish proportions. To inmates, it's still hellish, but much less of a mystery. Prison is like spending years in a torture chamber, but with a higher risk of catching a communicable disease. If we really wanted to punish people with something worse than flogging, we could sentence drug offenders to join gangs and fear for their lives; we could punish child abusers to torture followed by death; we could force straight men to have semiconsensual prison-gay sex. But we don't because we're better than that. Or at least we like to think so. All these things already happen, but we just sweep them under the rug and look the other way.

• • •

The numbers that describe the criminal justice system in America are not encouraging—but you didn't really think they would be, did you? In the nation's largest seventy-five counties, fifty-eight thousand defendants are charged with felonies each year, half of whom have multiple prior convictions. Of the accused, four in ten are charged with drug crimes, three in ten with property crimes, two in ten with violent crimes, and one in ten with a public order offense. Forty percent of suspects are kept in jail awaiting adjudication, while the rest pay bail or are released on their own recognizance (of those released, about a third get into more trouble before their case comes up).

Poor people, innocent and guilty alike, and even low-level nonviolent offenders languish in jail for days, weeks, and even years before their day in court. More than 10 percent of felonies take more than a year to resolve. But the majority of people in our jails have not been convicted of any crime. Jail is supposed to be for brief detentions before trial and for sentences of less than one year (sentences of more than a year are usually served in prison). If you have to pay bail—and through a bail-bond agent, you generally need to come up with only a fraction of the actual bail amount—you can pay and get out.

In New York City more than three-quarters of nonfelony defendants are released on their own recognizance. But of 19,000 misdemeanor cases with bail set at $1,000 or less, 16,500 did not post bail. No matter how low bail is set, if you don't have it, you stay in jail. The average stay for these minor offenders was sixteen days, which costs the city approximately $3,000 per person.

Every year millions of people like this get funneled through a very dysfunctional criminal justice system that is too overwhelmed to properly administer justice. Literally and figuratively, justice is plea-bargained. Given the capacity of our courtrooms, most cases *can't* go to trial. For serious crimes—prosecuted felony cases—fewer than one in twenty goes to trial. Baltimore City, where I worked, provides a typical example. The city's Circuit Court has ten thousand felony cases a year and the capacity to hold five hundred jury trials. Something has to give, so the system does its best to clear its caseload. In the seventy-five largest counties, about two-thirds of defendants accept a guilty plea, and most of the rest have the charges against them dropped. The small remainder are "diverted" (into drug treatment, for instance) or have "exceptional" outcomes (such as the suspect's death).

Nationwide, three-quarters of those who plead guilty to felony charges are given time behind bars. But with time served and a median sentence length of a year, simply saying you're guilty can allow you to walk free. If you refuse to accept a guilty plea— you might be innocent—you stay behind bars to wait your day in court. In a further Orwellian twist, some suspects spend more time in jail awaiting trial than the maximum possible time they could receive even if found guilty. Such can be life if you're poor and innocent and stubborn.

Of course it's not that everybody in jail is an innocent victim. People usually have some behavioral problems before they go to jail, but these problems just get worse behind bars. In jail people naturally fulfill the role expected of them. Consider Philip Zimbardo's notorious 1971 Stanford Prison Experiment. Two groups of college students were randomly assigned to play the role of either prisoners or guards in a make-believe prison experiment (it was pretty realistic in that students were "arrested" on the street and the prison was a refitted basement in the psychology department building). Both groups fell all too readily into their arbitrarily assigned roles: Students who were objectively similar just a few days earlier began acting like guards and prisoners. After only six days, the experiment had to be called off because "guards" were abusing "inmates," and some inmates were beginning to rebel, and others started to crack psychologically.

Almost as horrifying as what goes on in modern jails and how so many people wind up there is what happens after they're released. Whereas the process that sends so many Americans to prison is fundamentally defective, getting *out* of prison is equally problematic, albeit in different ways. Coming home after prison is called "reentry," and like every other stage of the criminal justice system, it fails. Just take the simple standard of making people not commit crime: Of the more than seven hundred thousand prisoners released each year, two-thirds are rearrested within three years, and half end up back in prison. Why? Maybe they're bad eggs. But even good eggs can do stupid things when they're without money, a stable home, antipsychotic medication, common sense, or the ability to find a job. Whatever circumstances led somebody to commit a crime probably haven't changed by the time they're freed. A released prisoner hangs out with the same friends in the same neighborhood and without the same job he never had. Or maybe a prisoner is a badass who enjoys adrenaline and the thrill of the crime.

Part of the problem is that not only do prisons not "cure" crime, they're truly criminogenic: Prisons *cause* crime. When released, people who go to prison are more likely to commit a crime than similar criminals who don't go to prison. This should be no surprise considering what happens when you group criminals together with nothing to do and all the time in the world. People make associations, form bonds, learn illegal skills, and reinforce antisocial norms.

Furthermore, to point out the obvious, criminals often come from neighborhoods with more crime. But what may not be obvious is the direction of the relationship between the two. It is not just that high-crime neighborhoods increase incarceration; high-incarceration neighborhoods also increase crime. Prisons and the war on drugs have turned entire neighborhoods into self-sufficient criminal creators. Currently, at some point in their lives, more than 50 percent of black men without a high school diploma do time in prison. Moreover, these men disproportionately come from very specific neighborhoods. A few years ago a researcher did an innovative analysis that highlights a phenomenon dubbed "million-dollar blocks." These are individual city blocks where more than $1 million is spent each year to incarcerate people from that block. Some particularly high-crime blocks require more than $5 million per year. This is money we're already spending, but poorly.

When too many young men from one neighborhood are in the criminal justice system, whether locked up or on probation or parole, the area reaches a tipping point, after which it can't function properly. When such a large segment of the population is sent away, everybody loses. Crime increases *because* a significant portion of the male population is not present. Of course there is a community benefit when a criminal menace is removed from the streets, but not all prisoners are menaces or will commit crimes all the time. And even bad people have some attributes that help their family and community function. From behind bars a prisoner can't be a father, hold a job, maintain a relationship, or take care of elderly grandparents. His girlfriend suffers. His baby's mother suffers. Their children suffer. Because of this, in the long run, we all suffer.

Consider the length of our sentences. There's no evidence that longer sentences deter crime. Unfortunately, we don't hear much of a call for shorter sentences for criminals. But the more time prisoners serve, the worse they and their job prospects will be upon release, and 95 percent of prisoners get released. What would happen if we just cut sentences in half? It's not too hard to imagine; Canada, just across the border, gives us a clue. The majority of all incarceration sentences in Canada are for less than one month. In Canada those convicted of "major assault" receive an average sentence of thirty-nine months. In America, however, the equivalent mean sentence for any violent offense is sixty-seven months. Shorter sentences are not the only reason for Canada's lower rates of crime and incarceration, but it's a small contributing factor.

In truth, even though very few people openly advocate that all prison sentences should be life sentences, all too often, that is essentially what happens. What would you do as a released felon? Get a job? On a job application there's a little box where you can write a paragraph to explain your felony conviction. Go ahead and write the best story you can, because it won't matter. When a potential employer asks if you've ever been convicted of a felony, there's a correct answer—and it's not "Yes, but. . . ." Given the choice between a convicted felon and a non-felon, why hire the felon? There's almost always a hard-working immigrant applying for the same job. And immigrants effectively get any criminal history expunged when they cross the border. Most of these immigrants do quite well, at least judging from the disproportionately few, compared to native-born Americans, who end up in prison. Maybe some US citizens deserve a similar clean slate.

Programs to help convicts reenter society are essential, but they don't receive the support they should. And they're too easy to target during budget cuts. Sometimes there's still lip service to helping prisoners, but it's usually nothing more than political rhetoric. Take California: In 2005 the Department of Corrections officially became the Department of Corrections and *Rehabilitation*. But there was no actual increase in rehabilitation. In New York State the Department of *Correctional Services* expresses the official desire to teach a mature work ethic through "positive individualized treatment plans." Really? Who goes to Attica or Sing Sing for vocational training? One of the few useful job skills that can be learned in prison is cutting hair, but it wasn't until 2008 that New York State allowed even nonviolent felons to get a barber's license. Most states still prohibit the practice.

After release, we want prisoners to work and become independent. But programs to help prisoners—such as assistance in finding jobs, paying rent, or finishing school—are a tough sell politically, especially when we don't offer similar benefits for noncriminals. And if some ex-con in a program, no matter how effective the program is, commits a newsworthy crime, the program is doomed. Reentry services are undercut at almost every turn, but without them, most released prisoners have little chance of staying out of jail.

New York's largest jail provides just one example of dysfunctional reentry. Rikers Island, which you can see while taking off or landing at LaGuardia Airport, can hold eighteen thousand inmates (though it's currently running under capacity). Let's say you get arrested for disorderly conduct in New York City. ("Dis-con," as it's known, is the general catch-all charge for disobeying or pissing off a police officer in New York. Every police department has a similar charge.) If this happens, you might spend a night or two on Rikers. If you've committed a real crime, you may be there much longer. Regardless, when your time is up, they'll take you on a white school bus to Queens Plaza South, just short of the bridge to midtown Manhattan. Getting off the bus by twelve lanes of traffic in the wee hours of the night (local business owners don't want prisoners released during business hours), you'll be greeted by a mixed crowd of loved ones, pimps, prostitutes, drug dealers, scam artists, strip clubs, and fried chicken joints. Hopefully you have somewhere to go or somebody is there to meet you. At this hour, the shelters are full or closed.

It's a sad day when the best-case scenario after getting out of jail is being homeless—but this is

reality. Only the most hopeful among us would seriously think a functionally illiterate broke man
with nowhere to go—and perhaps with substance-
abuse and anger-management issues to boot—is
going to turn his life around in the pre-dawn chill
at Queens Plaza. If he's like many offenders, he'll
do whatever crime comes best. To expect crime is
not to justify it, but really, what is the choice if
someone literally has nothing but the clothes they
were arrested in and a paper card worth two sub-
way fares?

Prison reentry causes a host of problems. Flogging, however, cleverly sidesteps these pitfalls because convicts don't enter prison in the first place.
Although flogging wouldn't alter the circumstances
that contribute to crime, at least it won't make
things worse. With flogging, one isn't derailed from
attempts to hold onto jobs, relationships, and housing. The lash may not set lives straight, but it would
at least give those who want to turn their lives
around more of a fighting chance.

• • •

I've never been incarcerated, and I don't personally
know anybody who is. I'm part of the country's

lucky half. For the other half, it's hard to imagine *not* knowing somebody behind bars. If you're poor or black or a high school dropout, you probably know people behind bars. If you're poor, black, *and* a high school dropout, there's a very good chance you *are* behind bars. If you commit a crime, no matter the crime, you're much more likely to end up behind bars if you're African American. All too often in this country race is a predictor for imprisonment. For any given crime committed, blacks are more likely than whites to be caught, jailed, prosecuted, convicted, or sentenced. This flies in the face of basic democratic principles of fairness—and yet it's a reality that many Americans have, astonishingly, learned to rationalize and accept.

Nationwide, about one-third of those behind bars are white. In New York City more than 80 percent of those arrested are minorities. But on Rikers Island 95 percent of those jailed are minorities. This is not to say that whites get handed a get-out-of-jail-free card, but because of how justice punishes the poor, this is essentially what happens. Nationwide there are more whites than blacks living under the poverty line, but the black poverty rate of 25 percent is twice as high as the white poverty rate. Of course we don't lock up people for being poor, but almost everybody we lock up is poor.

Given the poverty of the people filling our jails, it's almost as if we've reverted to a kind of eighteenth-century debtors' prison. In theory, our laws don't discriminate based on race or income, but think of the words from Anatole France's novel *The Red Lily*: "The law, in its majestic equality, forbids the rich as well as the poor to sleep under bridges, to beg in the streets, and to steal bread." To ask that the chances of a person being caught and punished for any given crime be roughly equal, regardless of race, would seem reasonable. If you do have to sleep under a bridge, beg in the streets, or decide to take drugs (not so many people steal bread these days), there's a greater chance you'll be arrested and incarcerated for it if you're black, especially when it comes to drugs, thanks in part to cruelly long mandatory sentences for crack cocaine. Survey after survey shows that compared to whites, blacks have similar if not lower levels of legal and illegal drug use. Yet in city after city, blacks are four, five, and even ten times more likely to be arrested for marijuana possession. The disproportionate incarceration of African Americans is partly due to increased poverty among blacks, partly due to higher rates of crime (particularly violent crime among young, black, male high school dropouts), partly because of greater police presence, and partly because the criminal justice system is unfair.

The racial problems in criminal justice can be traced back to two related practices: slavery and disenfranchisement. Slavery was a part of America before the country even existed. The nation's Founding Fathers were, to put it mildly, men of comfortable means. Although today a debate on slavery would be absurd and even offensive, back then many seemingly decent men argued in favor of slavery, or at least the postponement of its demise. There was even such a thing as antislavery slave owners. Take John Jay, the noted abolitionist and the first Supreme Court Chief Justice. Jay was lauded for buying slaves in order to free them, but he didn't free these men and women until they had worked off the purchase price. Better than nothing, I suppose, but the moral clarity at the time was as clear as mud.

The institution of slavery in the United States led to the subversion of any underlying democratic principles. Even after the United States gained independence and accepted that slavery would persist in the new, "free" republic, the Founding Fathers needed to figure out the nuts and bolts of political representation. In many states—take South Carolina, for instance, where 43 percent of residents were slaves—slavery would never have survived a democratic vote. So democracy was limited in order to perpetuate slavery.

What's more, the long-lasting if ultimately unsuccessful compromise (though it did last for over a century) was infamous. The Three-Fifths Rule stipulated that for the purposes of counting people to determine representation in government, slaves were three-fifths of a person. Slave owners, knowing full well that slaves wouldn't be allowed to vote, were the ones who disingenuously advocated full representation because any "representation" given to slaves would immediately pass into their masters' hands. Think about it: Under the Three-Fifths Rule, one man with five slaves held the political representation of four people (five, if you count his disenfranchised wife). After the first census in the United States, in 1790, Maine and Massachusetts were the only slave-free states. One in five Americans was a slave—numbers that surely made the newly empowered beneficiaries of the Three-Fifths compromise breathe a sigh of relief. After the Civil War, however, freed slaves made up about one-third of the South's population, and in Deep South states such as Mississippi and Louisiana, blacks were an absolute majority. This potential for political power threatened white supremacy, so many states simply denied blacks the basic rights of citizenship.

Disenfranchisement—to deprive people of the right to vote—is an essential principle in any apartheid state and was instrumental in codifying the postbellum repression of blacks. The effects of disenfranchisement were especially clear in a town in Wyoming County that had a population of six thousand, just half of whom were free. Unemancipated residents couldn't vote but nonetheless counted toward their white captors' political representation. Curiously, this particular community isn't even in a slave state, and even more disturbing, this situation lasted until 2010. Wyoming County is in New York, and the town in question is Attica, home of Attica Prison. In 2010 New York finally passed a state law to count prisoners, for representational purposes, as being from their home district. Until then, prisoners surrendered their political representation in the State House and US House of

Representatives to their mostly white captors in the prison's district.

Even when prisoners are counted in their home district for political representation, most can't vote, not even after being freed. In Florida more than 800,000 supposedly free men and women were prohibited from voting in the 2004 presidential election—a race decided by a few hundred votes— because of a past felony conviction. Nationwide 5.3 million Americans are denied the vote. Outcomes in small-town elections can be even more glaring. In Anamosa, Iowa, Danny Young was elected to the city council to represent 1,400 local people, just 58 of whom were not prisoners. When asked if he considered the prisoners to be his constituents, Mr. Young said, "They don't vote, so, I guess, not really." Young was elected with two votes—not by two votes, but *with* two votes (which, I should point out, is a troublesomely low voter turnout by any standard). The prisoners in his ward are denied any voice in their local government. I wouldn't be the first person to observe a transition in black America from slavery to segregation to incarceration. And although to say prison is modern-day slavery is a bit extreme, it seems as if some people never received Lincoln's proclamation about emancipation. Today, the population of incarcerated black men tops 850,000, most of whom cannot vote and many of whom will be legally disenfranchised for the rest of their lives.

Of course we cannot deny that corporal punishment, like prison, also has painful links to racism. Just as police dogs and fire hoses may forever be linked with Selma and Birmingham, whipping, a favored mode of punishment among slaveholders, carries particular symbolism that harks back to the darkest era in American history. Pictures of the terribly scarred backs of escaped slaves remain indelible stains on our nation's conscience—proof of our country's original sin. This horrific legacy of racism is troublesome, to say the least, but it is not in and of itself a valid reason to favor incarceration over corporal punishment. To argue against flogging because of past and present racism sorely misses the point. Indeed, flogging might even help illuminate racial injustice already present in the criminal justice system. When you enter any jail or prison in the United States you'll likely face a sea of black and brown faces. One can assume that the racial makeup of those being caned would be similar. But the inequities present in the status quo are not at all worsened by offering a choice of punishment.

If you're not convinced, think of the inverse. What if we currently had a system of flogging but no prisons? Would you be pleased with a book called *In Defense of Prisons*? In this book I could propose that rather than punishing convicts quickly and letting them get on with their lives, we could place these men and women in grim institutions far away from their homes and completely shut off from the outside world. Visitors, press, and all communication in and out would be restricted or heavily censored. And there they would stay for years. This would not be progress but instead the cruelest proposal of all. As a semipublic happening, flogging, for better and for worse, would air the dirty laundry of race and punishment in ways that prisons, by their very nature removed from society, cannot. To highlight an injustice is in no way to condone it. Quite the opposite.

• • •

The survival of mass incarceration can be traced, in no small degree, to the same kinds of economic pressures that once drove slavery itself. Incarceration is a business. In President Dwight Eisenhower's 1961 farewell address, he warned of a "military-industrial complex" that could control our national politics. And the "Prison-Industrial Complex" is a similar concept: not a conspiracy theory but rather a political confluence of various interest groups that benefit from the business of incarceration.

Poor rural districts see prisons not as an economic burden but as a lucrative market and potential employment opportunity. The cynical among us might even say we're spending billions of dollars to pay poor rural unemployed whites to guard poor urban unemployed blacks. In the 1980s New York Democratic Governor Mario Cuomo used a public agency to fund upstate prison construction in conservative Republican districts. The terrible irony about this particular agency, the Urban Development Corporation, is that it was created in 1968 to honor the legacy of Martin Luther King Jr. by building housing for the poor. Urban districts go along with prison building partly out of political necessity and partly because so many of their residents have been given, through prison, to rival districts.

Labor unions are another factor in prison construction; the various prison guard unions have always been major players in the prison-industrial complex. The California prison-guard union (euphemistically called the Correctional Peace Officers Association) represents thirty thousand workers in a $7-billion-a-year industry and has a war chest of about $22 million. It gives out money to politicians, literally and figuratively left and right. Being a correctional officer is a difficult job, and I've got nothing against unions. I myself am a union man (in a public-sector union, at that). I want unions to lobby for better pay and benefits and against prison privatization. But correctional officer unions should have no voice in lawmaking and sentencing policy. Doing so is an immoral and fiscal conflict of interest. When unions lobby to criminalize more people for longer times, prisons effectively become a new Works Progress Administration for our era, but without any of the constructive infrastructure, education, or culture. The horribly predictable results include more money going to incarceration than to higher education. Other effects of union clout are less obvious and even more devious. For instance, the California union gives money to local district attorneys' campaign funds. In at least two elections the union gave tens of thousands of dollars to the opponents of a district attorney who attempted to prosecute a guard for assault. Needless to say, there haven't been many prosecutions since.

In states without strong unions, private prisons are perhaps an even more devious player in the prison-industrial complex. In states with more influential unions, such as New York and Illinois, private prisons are prohibited altogether. But nationwide, private companies hold about 9 percent of the country's prisoners, generally in low- and medium-security institutions, which are cheaper and easier to manage. This web of corporations, shareholders, lobbyists, politics, and money is the prison-industrial complex in action. Now, some could argue that private prisons simply provide a needed service more efficiently than the government manages to. Others, myself included, cannot fathom how we give public money to private companies so they can profit from incarceration.

In truth, private prisons rarely save much money. The savings that do exist come mostly from labor; the average pay in private prisons is three-quarters of that found in public prisons. In 2009 the profits of CCA, the largest private prison company, were $155 million, or $5.35 per prisoner per day. If this money were not profit but wages split among the company's seventeen thousand employees, pay would increase to roughly the same level as unionized prison guards. One could say that prison corporations take public money from union workers and give it to private investors. Meanwhile, private-sector prison guards—faced with a starting salary between $11 and $13 an hour, limited benefits, and a very tough job—have a turnover rate of 40 percent annually.

Were private prisons simply providing a needed service in response to public demand, perhaps their use could be justified. But private prisons actively boost supply and then find ways to fill the beds. Take, for instance, the small town of California City, population nine thousand, in California's Mojave Desert. In 1996 CCA started building a 2,300-bed private prison purely on speculation; there was no guarantee the state would provide inmates. The president of the company predicted, "They'll avail themselves of it," while a local politician boasted,

"If we build it, they will come." They did build it, but the state of California, after intense union lobbying, did not provide any prisoners. Desperate, the company turned to the federal government and received federal prisoners, mostly immigrants in the country illegally who were facing deportation. Thinking about the four hundred additional jobs to guard these mostly nonviolent foreigners, the mayor exclaimed, "It's a trip." The city clerk expressed disappointment only in that the noncitizens wouldn't come quickly enough to count as official town residents in the 2000 census. In 2008, after losing a bid to a rival private prison company and threatened with closure, the California City Prison received another federal contract to fill the beds with immigrants. Meanwhile, the CCA and other private prison groups lobby for and even help draft tough anti-immigration laws, such as Arizona's controversial SB-1070.

If history is our guide, communities that depend on systems of human bondage for their economic well-being will not give up without a fight. Just as slaveholding communities exerted their outsized political influence to resist the abolition of slavery, so too will corporations and modern prison communities use their clout to stop penal reform and preserve the peculiar institution upon which their way of life depends. Flogging might be our best chance to break with the entire prison-industrial complex.

. . .

Profit and race are not the only factors associated with incarceration. Poverty, education, mental health, homelessness, addiction, one's neighborhood—these all have a huge impact on who goes to prison and who doesn't. When we ask prisons to function in a way for which they were never intended, the failure of incarceration becomes clear.

Think of a heroin addict arrested for drug possession—for the tenth time. Her guilt isn't in doubt. After all, she is an addict who buys and shoots up heroin every day. In front of the judge yet again, she is sentenced to probation and mandated treatment (which, not surprisingly, has a dismal failure rate—rehab works a lot better when people want to be clean). If she goes to jail, she loses any job she has and causes her family to suffer even more than they already do. Meanwhile, taxpayers pay for her jail, police overtime, the court's expenses, and perhaps even raising her children.

If the heroin addict's first nine arrests didn't set her straight, the tenth time is unlikely to be the charm—and yet in drug-related cases like these, we waste considerable expense pursuing a mode of punishment that is almost guaranteed to fail. Because we lead the world in illegal drug consumption, clearly we're doing something wrong. We know drug prohibition can't work; nevertheless, the mere possession of illegal drugs is grounds for arrest. Because of this, our criminal justice system is chronically overburdened. If it were up to me, I'd regulate, restrict, and tax drugs. I'd provide drug treatment for anybody who wants it. I also believe that what you put in your body should not be a government matter but something that concerns you, your family, and your doctor. Even if you disagree, admit that incarcerating people for drug possession is not making any problem go away.

Just as jails have effectively become our unofficial national rehab center, prisons are now our largest mental institutions. Certainly not all mentally ill people are criminals, nor are all criminals crazy, but more than half of all prisoners are classified as having mental health problems. That's not really surprising considering we're talking about incarcerated people. Who wouldn't have mental issues in prison? It's very much like Joseph Heller's original catch-22: To survive in prison you need to stay sane, but anybody who can stay sane in prison must be crazy. But more disturbingly, one-fourth of prisoners have a *history* of chronic mental illness, and two-thirds of these, 380,000 prisoners, were off their medications when they were arrested. Who knows how much crime we could prevent with proper mental health care? But the potential savings seem huge, both in terms of money and lives.

In fact, prisons today house far more of our mentally ill than do mental hospitals. In 1965 we had just 335,000 people in prison but 800,000 people in mental institutions. A lot of these "hospitals" were, in some ways—such as not being able to leave—very similar to prisons. Since 1965, however, the mental confinement rate has gone down 90 percent and the prison rate has increased fivefold. But it's not, as some people believe, that our prisons have simply taken the place of state-run mental hospitals. The two institutions never really catered to the same clientele; prisoners tend to be young, whereas most people in mental hospitals were much older. And thanks to Medicare, antipsychotic medicines, and general changes in attitudes toward the elderly and mentally ill, we don't need or want to confine as many noncriminals as we once did. If we still played by 1965 rules on detention, we would currently have roughly 1.8 million people in our mental and criminal institutions combined. That's still half a million fewer than we have in prison today.

Although the mentally ill population in our jails and prisons can't be singly attributed to the closing of mental institutions, mental institutions may have disappeared just a bit faster than did their need. There is without doubt a serious mental health crisis in our prison system. As the nation's greatest provider of mental health services, prisons don't provide very well. Certainly some of today's homeless would have been institutionalized back in the day. Left on the street, however, many get arrested, and health care in jail and prisons (especially jail) is notoriously bad. On top of that, one cannot imagine an environment less conducive to healing and mental health recovery than involuntary confinement surrounded by aggressive criminals—talk about a spiritual retreat from hell.

Just as we have adapted prisons to confine our mentally ill, a similar institution has come to house juvenile delinquents, with equally horrific consequences. The idea of having children sent to and kept in an institution—a practice known as juvenile detention, but really nothing more than incarceration for kids—began in 1825, when the House of Refuge opened in Manhattan. Like adult prisons, the nation's first juvenile prison didn't work very well. Press reports were, naturally, positive at first, but stories of kids being whipped and shackled soon reached the general public. Almost two centuries later, despite nearly two centuries of failure, the basic concept of juvenile detention persists. Perhaps, like with the penitentiary, people are happy to have others deal with their problems; troublesome people are out of sight and out of mind—picked up off the street and all but disappeared.

The horrors one finds in juvenile detention are particularly troubling because they happen to children, who make easier targets. We like to think of kids as more innocent than adults, or at least more redeemable. Instead, boys are routinely sedated with psychotropic medicines (and yet, for instance, New York State's juvenile homes don't have a single full-time psychiatrist on staff) and subject to the same physical and mental horrors as their older counterparts. The *New York Times* editorial staff recently felt compelled to come out against "young people being battered and raped in juvenile corrections facilities all across the country." One would hope such things go without saying, but apparently they don't. Twelve percent of youths in juvie homes reported being sexually victimized in the past year. In some juvenile facilities more than 30 percent of the boys say they're raped, mainly by staff members. Not surprisingly, self-inflicted injuries and suicide attempts are routine. We are warehousing our problem children in kiddie jail before they learn enough to graduate to adult prison.

And though the problems of juvie homes are really no different from those in any other system of incarceration, the financial costs of holding children are staggering. Leaving aside any costs associated with the actual crime and arrest, New York State spends more than $200,000 a year simply to detain and "treat" one child. And to what end? Ninety percent of released boys are rearrested by the time they're twenty-eight, and we probably lose track of the remaining 10 percent. As with prisons, it seems as if we're only willing to spend money on people after they mess up. Some of this $200,000 per year could be much better spent improving the lives of these children (and their poor parents) at a much earlier stage.

One significant reason that American prisons are so frequently misused these days—as drug treatment centers, juvenile penitentiaries, and housing for the mentally ill—is that we seem unwilling or unable to invest in people who may not be, to put it mildly, model citizens. If we're going to spend taxpayer money to prevent crime, spending it on people would be better than building more prisons. But this is not the choice America makes. We throw people in choppy waters and let them sink or swim. If they start to sink and curse us, we drag them out of the water and lock them up. We could just give them swimming lessons. In jail, violent offenders are mixed with immigrants who may have committed no crime other than crossing our border. We throw lifers in the same cell block as people who serve twelve months. Kids get raped. The mentally ill are left to fend for themselves in some antipsychotic medicinal haze. Given the impossible task of total control, some guards inevitably abuse their authority. Meanwhile, the taxpayer—the poor taxpayer—given no alternative, is forced to pick up the tab.

Houses of detention—prisons, jails, juvie homes, mental institutions . . . call them what you will—have failed unequivocally at the basic tasks we've set out for them because people who aren't free want first and foremost to be free. Personal improvement and everything else comes later. But without rehabilitation, prisons have few other purposes. One is incapacitation, the idea of keeping criminals away from the rest of us. Another is punishment, intended for retribution and also deterrence, both for the offender and any others who may contemplate similarly nefarious deeds. If we were to grade prisons at these functions—rehabilitation, incapacitation, and punishment/deterrence—the only good grade comes from incapacitation: Here prisons get a gold star. Through technology, experience, and an unhealthy dose of inhumanity, we've pretty much mastered the art of keeping people behind walls. But for the vast majority of these people, prison neither rehabilitates nor deters. And when it comes to getting an apartment, a job, or college aid, the concept of "having done one's time" and getting on with life no longer exists. A felon is a felon for life. So prisons warehouse criminals, whether they be rich, poor, white, or black—but mostly poor and nonwhite.

Institutionalization—in prisons, asylums, and public housing—has effectively created a disposable class of people to be locked away and discarded. This was not always the case. Historically, even though great efforts were made in early America to keep "outsiders" and the "undeserving" poor off public welfare rolls, society's undesirables—the destitute, disabled, insane, and even criminals—were still considered part of the community. The proverbial village idiot may have been mocked, beat up, and even abused, but he was still the *village's* idiot. Some combination of religious charity, public duty, and familial obligation provided (not always adequately) for society's least wanted. Then reformers got involved. Although designed in part to benefit the public in a free and self-governing society, the almshouse, orphanage, public hospital, and prison all shared a similar and more nefarious purpose: to effectively manage and remove society's least wanted.

In the colonial era exile as a punishment was a last resort, and a severe one at that. Prisons, whether or not it was their intention, brought back exile—but now as the first and, in many cases, only resort. In being, as a contemporary observer aptly described Newgate Prison, "unseen from the world," prisons severed the essential link between a community and punishment. Public punishment and shame became isolation and containment. Without being visible, convicts went from being part of "us"—the greater community—to a more foreign "them." So now we wait for the troubled and unproductive to break the law. And then we hold them for months and years, again and again, until they age out of crime or die. This is what happens when we take traditional punishment such as flogging out of the arsenal. We've run out of options.

Certainly for some, prison has a place in our society. A few people need to be locked up because we're afraid of what they'll do to us. Pedophiles, psychopathic killers, and terrorists immediately come to mind. Hannibal Lecter may be the most well-known case study of a man who needs to remain behind bars (albeit a fictional one, lest we forget); his real-life equivalents—such as Jeffrey Dahmer, John Wayne Gacy, Willie Bosket, Theodore Kaczynski, Khalid Shaikh Mohammed—may indeed need to be kept away from us as long as they are alive. We're afraid of them. These people are not only being punished for what they did; they're being kept behind bars so they can't hurt us anymore. For these nasty folk—mind you, they're few and far between—prisons contain and do so rather well. But prisons and jails are not filled with monsters; rather, they're filled with a lot of mediocre people— a very few bad ones too—who did something wrong, and often did that something more than once.

Sometime in the past few decades we seem to have lost the concept of justice in a free society. Now we settle for simple efficiency of process. We tried rehabilitation and ended up with supermax and solitary confinement. Crime, violence, and drug prohibition help explain why so *many* people are behind bars. But none of this explains why there are so many people *behind bars*. That fact represents a much deeper problem, one that we have yet to confront. If we can't guarantee some degree of public safety while providing a minimal level of humanity for those we shackle; if justice isn't the goal;

if we're not willing to invest in education, rehabilitation, mental health care, infrastructure, job creation, or troubled neighborhoods, then we have no choice: It's time to short-circuit the entire criminal justice system by bringing back the lash.

• • •

Although the prison system is unarguably broken, many people have yet to acknowledge that the problem is the system itself and not just the way it's run. Today's prison reformers still seem to believe, or at least want to believe, that the problem of prisons rests more in the details of prison administration than the basic tenets of the penitentiary model. To attack prisons in their entirety, reformers would have to abandon the penitentiary's restorative ideals—something they're loath to do. Though the idea of rehabilitative prisons may have officially been abandoned with the Supreme Court's 1989 *Mistretta* decision, reformers still cling to the concept that prisons can reform. Their reluctance to let go is understandable. Like education, job training, and drug treatment, rehabilitation is tough to be against. What's the alternative? Still, the premise of rehabilitation is often flawed. How, after all, can one be "habilitated" in the mainstream values and skills of the educated working class when isolated from them in a "total institution" while surrounded by undereducated criminals with similar antisocial attitudes? Gathering criminals in one place does nothing but teach advanced criminality. If rehabilitation is to ever work, it's going to happen outside prison walls.

Without the noble ideal of rehabilitation, prisons only hold and punish. And as a system of punishment, prisons leave much to be desired. Despite the horrid conditions, many people continue to believe that penitentiaries do nothing but coddle criminals. After all, some critics argue, with rent-free recreation and cable TV, prison is a veritable country club! As common as it is misguided, this belief causes the public to demand even more punishment. Elected officials respond by getting "tougher" on crime. But without alternatives, tougher just means more prison.

No matter how tough we get, because prisons do not punish in a comprehensible manner, incarceration will never satisfy the public's legitimate desire for punishment. But when incarceration is all we have, the only way to give more punishment is to pile on the years. Without satisfactory punishment, the public brays for more punishment. And so the cycle continues. Ten years not enough? Give him twenty! Why? Because he *deserves* it. Consider convicted felons Dudley Kyzer and Darron Anderson. The former received ten thousand years *plus* two life terms for a triple murder; the latter received twenty-two hundred years for rape, kidnapping, and robbery. A judge, on an appeal by Mr. Anderson, added nine thousand years to his sentence (a second appeal knocked off five hundred years). Mr. Anderson's release is set for the year 12744. Clearly, this is absurd.

If you think that "getting tough on crime" works, that if only we added enough years and made incarceration bad enough, then nobody would risk committing crimes, please meet Sheriff Joe Arpaio of Maricopa County, Arizona. Sheriff Joe, who likes to be known as "America's Toughest Sheriff," is proud of the harsh conditions in his jail: striped uniforms, pink underwear, chain gangs, sleeping in tents, no coffee, and cheap food. Arpaio proudly says his feedings cost just twenty-two cents per person per meal, twice a day. But it's not just about frugality. Arpaio says prisoners deserve to be punished: "I don't want criminals to be happy and comfortable in my jail. If you don't want to be there, don't commit the crime." Fair enough—until we consider that 70 percent of his inmates are technically innocent "pretrial detainees." When jail is used for pretrial detention, it is supposed to hold, not punish. But perhaps more important than Arpaio's inability to understand legal nuances is that his much-touted "get tough" policies don't work, at least not in any way that deters crime or prevents recidivism.

A few years back Arpaio commissioned a study to examine and highlight his successes. Two recruited professors looked at people sentenced and released from his jail before and after Sheriff Joe was elected. But their findings don't support Arpaio. They found no difference in the recidivism between offenders released before Sheriff Joe took over and those released a few years later, after he "got tough" and introduced his unique brand of hospitality. Nor has Arpaio deterred other people from getting into trouble. Since he took over, the jail's population has more than doubled, to ten thousand prisoners.

Honestly, though, the recidivism rate probably means little to Arpaio and his numerous fans

(Arpaio has won by a wide margin every election since 1993). For these people the issue is less about facts and figures than a deep-rooted desire to punish criminals. But it would be nice if those who advocated get-tough approaches would at least be honest and say their policies are more about vengeance than preventing crime. In an era when ignoring data and being contradicted by so-called "libs" is a rite of passage for conservative politicians, Sheriff Joe and his supporters simply discount any opponents as politically biased.

In the study of Arpaio's effectiveness, the Arizona professors started with the premise that for get-tough policies to deter, inmates must actually dislike the policies. And although Arpaio's gimmicks may garner contempt from liberals and applause from conservatives, in truth they may matter very little. The professors interviewed hundreds of inmates about their attitudes toward Arpaio's jail. Inmates disliked being incarcerated, but beyond that, Arpaio's policies garnered little hatred.

Regardless of anything happening in jail, a third of the inmates believed they'd be back no matter what. The real-life conditions that led them to crime in the first place—mentioned most were alcohol, drugs, inability to pay child support, and not having a driver's license needed to get to work—weren't going to change upon their release. Among other inmates with more long-term plans to stay out of jail, the most complained-about aspects of incarceration were hardly unique to Maricopa County: lack of recreation, cold food, group quarters, and cigarette bans. It doesn't matter what color the underwear is—jail is jail. The "toughness" Arpaio has tried to bring to his jail may pale in comparison with the fundamental hardships of most prisoners' lives.

Indeed, the political camps for and against Sheriff Joe may be staked out on the wrong side of his policies. The irony about a man who says, "I want to make it so terrible that nobody will want to come back" is that deep down, and without him wanting it, some of his policies might not be bad. Tent cities, even in an Arizona summer, can be preferred to stuffy indoor cells. Inmates dismissed chain gangs ("work crews" is the politically correct term) as publicity stunts, and yet whatever their symbolism, they remain highly desired assignments. And the reason should be obvious: Inmates will welcome anything that provides an emotional and physical release from the monotony of confinement.

Unfortunately, by attacking the ideas of Joe Arpaio, his more liberal opponents may be hurting the very inmates in whose name they claim to speak. Time and time again we see that inmates don't want to be locked inside. Any and every alternative to wasting away in a jail should be heralded, no matter who it comes from. Plus, I'm quite fond of some of his ideas, like the one linking TV power to electricity-generating exercise bicycles. If you want to watch the tube, keep pedaling. Why not?

Not liking Joe Arpaio is one thing. After all, *I* don't like Joe Arpaio. I think he's an egotistical, xenophobic, opportunistic SOB. There are better ways to punish criminals than a "get tough" jail. But until we provide alternatives and acknowledge the necessity of punishment, true reform will be a pipe dream and we'll be left with Arpaio's gimmicks. So I raise my middle finger to you, Joe, but urge you to keep the ideas coming.

• • •

If prisons are broken, then so, too, is prison reform. With the exception of a few Supreme Court decisions in their favor, prison reformers have an awfully bad track record over the past two hundred years.

But the last forty years stand out as particularly dismal: Calls for less incarceration have been met with a skyrocketing prison population. This, however, isn't surprising, as any reform movement that desires an improved system of evil *should* be doomed to failure. It's like asking for comfier seats on the train to Auschwitz: It sort of misses the big picture.

At one time America had punishment other than incarceration. But as we built up our prison system in the nineteenth and twentieth centuries, we simultaneously dismantled our most trusted alternative: the institution of flogging. In 1972 Delaware, the country's "first state," became the last to strike corporal punishment from the criminal code. This was twenty years after the state's last flogging. On June 16, 1952, convicted burglar John Barbieri, aged thirty, was tied to "Red Hannah," as the whipping post was known, and received twenty lashes on the back with the "cat-o'-nine-tails." Seeing how every other state had already given up flogging, perhaps Delaware's stubborn refusal in keeping the lash was due to its proximity to and rivalry with neighboring Pennsylvania, where flogging was first banned and the prison movement began.

In the debate between flogging and prison, both sides saw prison as the "softer" of the two options. The only real question was which one was better. Anti-floggers in the late 1700s saw prison as a modern cure for crime. But the pro-flogging Delaware *Gazette* saw through this nonsense: "The Penitentiary punishment," wrote the *Gazette* in 1852, "scarcely ever reforms the criminal, and we believe that it is much less efficient than our old fashioned mode of whipping and pillory."

A stated goal of the pro-prison camp was nothing less than the complete elimination of criminal punishment. In its place would be scientific treatment. One anti-flogging academic in 1947 quite typically hoped for an "emphasis upon the understanding of the causes of crime [and] the rehabilitation of the individual. . . . [Focus] upon the criminal rather than upon the crime, upon the person in a situation rather than upon"—and here's the kicker—"legal abstractions." Of course these "legal abstractions" are nothing less than an independent judiciary, the Bill of Rights, and the rule of law. But at least this professor was honest, just one in a long line of misguided dreamers seduced by the curative ideals of the penitentiary. It remains important, both logically and morally, to resist the seduction of these utopian dreams.

Prison reform, somewhat like communism, has in its idealism a certain enduring appeal—especially if all you know about communism is *The Communist Manifesto* and a rousing round of "The Internationale." In some circles even today, prison reformers' beliefs, much like those of communism, reflect a dogmatic faith that an ineffectual system can be salvaged to help society improve. This wouldn't matter so much if these were lofty statements of ideals, like, say, wanting world peace. In reality, however, advocates impose their dreams on millions of people with catastrophic effects. Just like early communists who wanted a more just world, one might forgive the early Quaker prison advocates who didn't yet know the horrific consequences of their ideas. But for modern reformers to maintain a utopian vision of incarceration that flies in the face of two centuries of real-world failure is inexcusable. True believers, by and large, never admit failure. They just try harder.

Let's look at some of the theoretical parallels between prison and communism. First, both began with noble ideals. Communism was supposed to let the hard-working masses throw off their chains of oppression; prisons were intended to cure criminals. But just as Marx built his theory on shaky pilings (such as the assumption that people actually want to work), the ideological foundation of the penitentiary system rests on the loopy theory that specially enlightened professionals can "cure" criminals. Additionally, both prison and communism rely on theories of mandatory "reeducation" toward some administrative or party line. Finally, both communism and prison have been tried in many forms and variations, none of which have succeeded by any democratic standard (hence walls to keep people in). Technically, of course, saying something does not work is not the same as saying that something *could not* work, but constant failure, especially when we're experimenting on real people, should give more freedom-loving and ethically inclined people serious pause.

Perhaps the hearts of early prison reformers were in the right place. But the same could be said, in another unusual comparison, of Dr. Victor Frankenstein. The doctor was a smart man—undoubtedly charming at times—even if perhaps a bit eccentric at committee meetings. Dr. Frankenstein did not want to create a monster. Based on his beliefs about human nature, he wanted to create life from death. But unlike most prison advocates, the good doctor was quick to realize the potential danger of his creation: "Now that I had finished, the beauty of the dream vanished, the breathless horror and disgust filled my heart. . . . Mingled with this horror, I felt the bitterness of disappointment: dreams that had been my food and pleasant rest . . . were now . . . a hell to me." Like Frankenstein's beast (at least in the movie version), the prison monster has escaped and taken on a life of its own, and is wreaking havoc. It needs to be destroyed—though preferably not by a mob with flaming torches—and replaced with some more natural, manageable, and human system.

But, you may protest, just because our prisons are a mess doesn't mean we should adopt something as horrible as flogging! If we were willing to tax more and spend wisely, we too, like most of Western Europe, could have a decent economy, good public schools, paid vacation, longer lives, less violence, shorter prison sentences, and an incarceration rate that's a fraction of what we have now. So it's with a tinge of regret and envy that I note, of course, that this is not our system. Americans like guns, cowboys, individualism, and being tough. If American politicians can lose votes by seeming to enjoy European pleasures, true European-style socialism and radical penal reform have no chance.

Yes, we could do better with what we have, but in the real world of deficits, budget cuts, victims' rights groups, and correctional officers' unions, money that could be spent elsewhere or saved will almost invariably not be spent helping criminals. As long as politicians tarred as "soft on crime" lose elections, essential criminal justice reform will go nowhere. Prison reform is a noble goal, but at the end of the day it's just another pie-in-the-sky dream—and one that, by attempting to repair a fundamentally irreparable system, causes millions of Americans to suffer with more of the status quo.

The ghastly nature of involuntary incarceration makes it even more imperative that we differentiate between reality and fantasy. Why not improve our criminal justice services? Why not, indeed? And while we're at it, let's fix our schools, courts, public transportation, and health care. We could even eliminate or fix the death penalty—after all, it's also a mess! Crime would go down because people with doctors, meds, and enough money to get by generally don't go out robbing and killing. And undoubtedly, if parents did a better job raising their children, there would be fewer future adults to punish.

In the meantime, please show me an effective court system that convicts actual offenders and protects the innocent, or a humane prison that houses only the guilty. Show me an enlightened jail that takes in our poorest, meanest, and most desperate and churns out hardworking, industrious taxpayers. You can't. Nor will you ever. Only in a utopian world can we rehabilitate criminals, and our vision for the future should not be blinded by a Big Rock Candy Mountain mirage where handouts grow on bushes and the lakes are filled with stew.

There is some good news, however: Finally, after four decades of unprecedented increase, in much of the nation (though not all of the nation), prison growth has essentially stopped. This is a thin silver lining to cloudy economic times. Most states are trying to figure out ways to reduce incarceration costs, which can be done by everything from skimping on meals to closing entire institutions. Three big states—New York, New Jersey, and Texas—have managed to reduce the number of people incarcerated, and indeed, by the time you read this, there is a good chance that, after an incredible forty-year run, fewer Americans will be incarcerated than were in the previous year. I hope so, and if so, great. But signs that prison growth has stopped should not be cause for celebration. It's setting the bar way too low. Keeping 2.3 million people incarcerated is wrong.

We live in a nation that incarcerates more of its population than any other, and that includes authoritarian China (which has an incarceration rate of 180 per 100,000, including political prisoners), theocratic Iran (220), and communist Cuba (530). America's incarceration rate, 750, is five times the world's average. Other than Cuba, the only countries that even come close to America are Russia (629) and Rwanda (604). This is not good company to be in. Democratic countries we're less ashamed to compare ourselves to—England, France, Germany, Spain, Canada—all have incarceration rates nearer to 100. Interestingly, for most of the twentieth century, so did the United States.

We might consider 100 per 100,000 a somewhat "natural" rate of incarceration—if there were such a thing. From 1860 to 1904 the American incarceration rate increased from 60 to 110 per

100,000. And there it remained, give or take, until the 1970s and the war on drugs. A few people are so dangerous they need to be confined and kept away from us, but that number is probably closer to Japan's incarceration rate of 60 than America's 750.

Despite our astonishingly high rates of incarceration, there is still an active pro-prison camp that wants to build more prisons. When not talking about job creation for economically disadvantaged white communities, these people fall back on the smug assertion that we need to keep locking up more people as long as more people keep violating the law. But for consensual crimes—such as drug use, in which there are no victims—what is gained from incarceration?

What we have in America is a massive, terrifying, and out-of-control experiment in incarceration. Our system has effectively become a gulag—a model that cannot coexist with a free and civilized nation. And only when reformers confront this harsh reality will we be able to stop tinkering with our broken system and move on to something, such as flogging, that works better, or at least does less harm.

• • •

In twenty-first-century America, could we have court-sanctioned flogging? It's unclear, but it's not currently prohibited. The Supreme Court has never explicitly ruled on the matter, and until it does, we should assume it's constitutional. There is some interesting precedent (which some mistakenly believe bans flogging), such as *Jackson v. Bishop.* This 1968 Court of Appeals decision was very unsympathetic to corporal punishment but only banned whippings in the context of prison discipline—and thus ended the practice of prison wardens carrying around whips. But prison discipline is not the same as legally sanctioned criminal punishment. Discipline is at the discretion (and potential abuse) of a warden and issued for administrative violations, whereas court-sanctioned criminal punishment follows law and due process and has constitutional safeguards.

Additionally, the Supreme Court has since noted that though it affirmed *Bishop*, that case has never been "embraced by the Court." In other words, don't read too much into the lesser court's decision, especially with regard to precedent. The Supreme Court has since, in the 1977 *Ingraham v. Wright*, upheld the right of public schools to use corporal punishment (in some ways the same punishment *Bishop* said may not be used in prison), and twenty-two states still permit corporal punishment in school. But the Court's pro-flogging decision in *Ingraham* was more technical than philosophical, based on the grounds that constitutional criminal justice protections, such as due process and prohibitions against cruel and unusual punishment, do not extend to schoolchildren.

Given the more conservative makeup of the present Supreme Court (and the fact that it is still constitutional for principals to beat disobedient schoolchildren), it's not hard to imagine judicial flogging could pass constitutional muster. Although one unexpected "no" vote might come from conservative Justice Antonin Scalia, who wrote, "I cannot imagine myself, any more than any other federal judge, upholding a statute that imposes the punishment of flogging." Another "no" vote is more predictable, coming from liberal Justice Stephen Breyer, who said, "Flogging as a punishment might have been fine in the 18th century. That doesn't mean that it would be OK, and not cruel and unusual, today." Breyer embraces the idea that constitutional standards of punishment evolve over time. Were flogging found to violate Eighth Amendment prohibitions against cruel and usual punishment, the 1957 decision *Trop v. Dulles*, which invoked "the evolving standards of decency that mark the progress of a maturing society," would assuredly come into play.

In any event, the matter of flogging's constitutionality may, in the end, be moot. In my proposed flogging no one is ever forced to be flogged. And the court hears only cases in which a victim has suffered actual harm. Just as people can waive certain constitutional rights—such as the right to a jury trial when accepting a guilty plea—they might likewise willingly cede protection from cruel and unusual punishment if flogging were, in fact, found to be cruel and unusual. With the consent of the flogged, flogging would simply be an option— probably a popular one—in lieu of the status quo. It is difficult to argue that giving a choice to the convicted is morally or constitutionally indecent.

To flog with consent is key. Without consent, caning could indeed be torturous, cruel, and unusual. With consent, however, many illegal, dangerous, and even stupid activities become acceptable: boxing, mixed martial arts, BASE jumping, bull riding, sadomasochism, figure-eight car racing, and, of course, sex—which does, for some, include flogging. Almost anything that involves adults that does not actually kill becomes legal with consent (though there are a few peculiar exceptions, such as drug possession, having sex for money, and working for less than minimum wage).

However, some would oppose flogging precisely *because* it is an option. If I were speaking at my college about the horrors of prison and the need for change, some conservative student, perhaps a police officer, would raise a hand and say, "This is exactly why we need prison. Flogging is too soft! We shouldn't give criminals any more choice than they gave their victim!" Now, no matter your belief about the severity of prison—whether you think that prison is an almost indescribably hideous institution or a luxury resort—please understand that prison may be too hard or too soft, but it can't be both. I call this the Goldilocks Dilemma.

Every conscientious reader should confront the question of which is harsher: prison or flogging. Not that punishment should be judged by harshness alone, but how you assess their comparative harshness has very real consequences as to how we proceed. If we as a society cannot even reach consensus about what prison *is*, how can we ever discuss what needs to be done? And even if we can't agree which form of punishment is harsher, in order to have any discussion at all—be it on prison reform, overhauling the entire penal system, or just kicking up our heels and doing nothing—we can at least agree that prison and flogging have different degrees of harshness.

I hope you agree that flogging, harsh though it is, is a far better choice than prison. And if you think, as I suspect some do, that both prison and flogging are cruel but flogging is still beyond the pale, then ask yourself why you would choose the lash for yourself to avoid prison and yet still refuse to give that choice to others. If you wouldn't choose the lash for yourself, I may never convince you that flogging is a better option (though I appreciate you reading this far), but hopefully you've been convinced that prison is not the answer.

If you think flogging lets people off too easily, we could debate the appropriate number of lashes. But if you think flogging should not be a choice because it's not cruel enough, if your opposition to flogging is based on the idea that whipping is too soft, if you want all convicts to suffer the worst possible pain imaginable (including but not limited to rape and insanity), if you think prisons are great precisely because they torture so cruelly and horribly, then you need to take a deep look at your own humanity, because you might be a very evil person.

• • •

Violence may seem an unsavory alternative to prison, but punishment must by definition hurt in some way, be it emotionally, psychologically, monetarily, or physically. Punishment must cause pain. Physical violence has the advantage of being honest, inexpensive, and easy to understand. For many Americans violence is part of life. It is not incomprehensible that when softer cajoling and rational persuasion fail, corporal discipline, or at least the threat of it, is an effective deterrent and can even make a substantial difference on the course of a person's life. For many children growing up in disadvantaged neighborhoods, the challenge isn't to follow the social norms of one's peers but to actively resist them. Many of my students tell me they wouldn't be in college if not for corporal punishment. More interesting is that they tell me they're eternally grateful for this discipline. These are college students making it. Without grandpa's belt, they tell me, or at least the threat of it, they'd be in the streets, in prison, or dead.

I don't mean to defend child abuse or unprovoked violence, but wishing away violence is not the solution. Two dozen nations have even gone so far as to outlaw parental spanking, even in the home, often on the assumption that physical discipline equals or inevitably leads to child abuse. By American standards a ban on spanking is extreme, but whatever standards one uses, this resistance to violence is not entirely logical. Far too many who oppose corporal punishment can be a bit clueless about the fundamental realities in so many people's lives. Our society has a homicide rate three times that found in Western Europe and an imprisonment rate seven times higher. We don't get these disgraceful realities from being pacifist (which is too often a luxury of the well-off). This is a tough country, and sometimes, even if it's not ideal, order is maintained through force, or at least the threat of retaliation. Those with more means may scorn such a violence-dependent life, but those with more means can pay other people, such as police officers, to do their violence for them.

Certainly, for good and bad, violence can have a lasting impact. I still remember when I was in third grade and some kid I didn't even know hit me. For no reason. He just came up and punched me. Bam! As a wronged eight-year-old, my first re-action was to find the nearest adult—who happened to be a worker, not a teacher—and mustered up all the righteous indignation I could. "He hit me!" I said, looking up expectantly while a large woman gazed down with a quizzical look. Her four words still ring in my ears: "Well . . . hit him back!"

Hit him *back*?

The thought of hitting him back had not oc-curred to me. I was a naive kid and I wasn't raised that way. So I did nothing. I never saw that other kid again. Looking back, I suppose I got punked, but if your upbringing was similar to mine, maybe you don't even know what getting "punked" or being "dissed" means. Or maybe, if you are a bit more street-savvy but more mature, you do know these words but still find the concepts quite laugh-able. If some stranger bumps into you or steps on your shoes or even straight-up insults you, you might just laugh it off. Why up the ante over a perceived slight and risk trouble? You have too much to lose. You're above it. You can always walk away.

But what if you get disrespected every time you leave the house? Is it ever okay to hit back? There's a simple rule that many people live by: Those who do wrong deserve to be beat. It may not be the most enlightened strategy, and maybe you disagree, but it is tried and true. And somewhat disturbingly, it probably works better than jail. But outside of self-defense and limited parental discipline, you're really never legally allowed to hit somebody. Although too much violence is admittedly very bad, it doesn't necessarily follow that a little is a terrible thing.

Violence can be an important tool, especially when used as a last resort. Twenty years after I got hit in third grade, when I was working as a police officer on the rough streets of Baltimore, I didn't have a chip on my shoulder or a grudge to settle. But I knew I couldn't get punked. For a police officer, it isn't safe. An unanswered threat one day is a potential threat every day to come. Passivity invites danger and can get you killed, and so police officers have to adopt a "hit him back" mentality. "Don't fight the police," a friend's father said. "They're not in the habit of losing." Admittedly, I'm not a brawler. Quite the opposite. But still, like all police, I needed to be able to prove my authority. Without an "or else!"—without the threat of force—people won't do what they need to do, even if a police officer is the one doing the telling.

But because police can't use force all the time, they rely on locking people up. Arrests, however, haven't always been the main tool in the law enforcement kit. Like many police, I heard stories from my fellow officers about policing in the "good old days"—which you've always just missed—when some minor offenders would be given a choice between handcuffs or a minor beat-down. Given a choice between a night in jail and going out back and taking a punch or two, most offenders, I was told, stoically (if not happily) chose the more honorable "beat and release" over the indignity of a night in Central Booking.

By the time I hit the streets, the "beat and release," or crimes "abated by beating," were already history. Word undoubtedly came down from above that corporal (and illegal) alternatives to incarceration were no longer acceptable. But without a corporal option, there's no middle ground between letting someone go and locking him up. So instead of hitting back, police arrest. That was fine by me because I wasn't raised to hit back. But now, for something minor, instead of a warning or a crack on the head, a disrespectful kid gets locked up. Instead of a lump and a lesson, the hoodlum has to deal with too-tight handcuffs, a strip search, hunger, boredom, being surrounded by criminals, a temperature in jail that is always too hot or too cold, and an arrest record. Is that progress?

Back in the day, or so I've been told, police might beat a wife beater. Consider this recollection of a long-retired Atlanta police officer, lamenting the demise of old-school policing:

> I miss those days before Rodney King. Back then you could roll up on a scene, domestic or just some street drama, and you *know* who the bad guy is. No *Law & Order* bullshit, no big mystery. He knew it, you knew it, and he knew that you knew it. You simply ask him the question: Do you want to go to jail or do you want to settle it right here? Most would take the medicine right there. You give them a bit of a thumping and go on your way. Nothing excessive,

nothing truly abusive. The street had a feel for how much was the right dose and if you were good you would work within that.

Alas, not all police are good, and extralegal authority can easily be abused, but that does not negate the potential benefits of legal and consensual corporal punishment.

Now police have no choice but to lock up offenders, especially in cases of domestic assault, where mandatory arrest laws all but cuff the police. Laws such as these, which limit discretion, are a good example of good intentions run amok. If a couple fights, police simply lock up the winner. Any sign of injury means somebody is going to jail. Period. End of story. But of course that never really is the end of the story. Jail never is. Logically, different situations require different responses. This is why we pay and train police officers. When we take away discretion, we make things worse.

Once I responded to a domestic call after a man came home, admitted to catting around, got yelled at, and earned a big fat lip when his wife slugged him. He deserved it, he told me (and he probably did). But while his wife was yelling, neighbors called the police. Guess what? She went to jail. That's the way it is—mandatory arrest for domestic violence—that's what the law says. In other instances, a girlfriend who had been beaten would point to her kids and beg me not to take away the babies' working father. But I had no choice. If I didn't make an arrest and then something happened, it would be on me. A week later, I'd be back at the same home for another fight, only now he was unemployed, having lost his job from the earlier arrest. Still later, such couples would often show up in court all lovey-dovey to have the charges dropped. These people needed help, but it wasn't going to come from me. Of course police still have some discretion, but when it comes to punishing wrongdoing, the only legal option is to arrest. But arrests don't work. The same people get locked up again and again for the same crime.

When I policed in Baltimore, there were one hundred thousand arrests a year, with twenty thousand of those happening in the district I patrolled. That's a lot of arrests, especially for an area with fewer than forty-five thousand people. In such neighborhoods, police arrest on a massive and almost incomprehensible scale. Who benefits from these arrests except the lawyers, police, and correctional officers who get paid? Of course there is plenty of serious crime, and sometimes you need to slap on the cuffs. But the bulk of arrests are for minor things—things that people in better neighborhoods usually get away with—drinking, drug possession, disorderly conduct, loitering, and even simple assault.

Maybe the old option of the "beat and release" wasn't so bad. Compared to court, police punishment can be quicker, more proportionate, and even more consistent—the three factors that just happen to meet Beccaria's original concept of deterrence. The bygone system of discretion and giving a choice made sure some minor offenders received a less destructive option than building a rap sheet. "You know," a friend of mine, a retired ranking African American police officer, said:

> When I was growing up in Baltimore, police would whup your ass. I don't think that was such a bad thing. I'm pro–corporal punishment. But the thing is, police would know you and who your parents were. If your parents would beat you, they'd just hand you over. But if there was no discipline at home, they would take you

somewhere and work you over. It worked. Certainly better than it works today. At least after a beating you had essentially a clean slate. And a good lesson. What happens today is a joke. You just go through the system and come out the other end. Where's the lesson in that? It just teaches you the system doesn't care.

So rather than take flogging off the table as punishment, it would be better to wipe incarceration from the debate and then figure out the best way to administer justice.

Just as my friend was familiar with the concept of "beat and release" well before he became a police officer, most of the people I arrested were no strangers to old-fashioned beat-downs. The rules were simple because that way everybody understands. If we don't punish wrongdoers, the worst among us will keep doing wrong. Many didn't seem to mind the basic concept, at least in response to wrongdoing. For a lot of people, violence is nothing more than a fact of life. You get your butt kicked and move on. It happens. The world, or at least their world, was a violent place. People in rough neighborhoods develop attitudes and toughness as survival mechanisms not because they're bad people but because they don't have other resources on which to rely. Different environments may require different attitudes toward discipline, parenting, and social control—different strokes for different folks, if you will.

Because corporal punishment may often be preferable to arrest, why not offer flogging as a legalized form of the old "beat and release"? In the long run, a criminal conviction is far more damaging than a violent but brief lashing. It might be a crazy world when flogging is a better choice than what we now call "justice," but over a lifetime, for instance, a typical released inmate will earn 40 percent less than a similar nonincarcerated person. Flogging is brutal—hell, flogging is supposed to be brutal—but brief, intense pain is better than long, drawn-out confinement. Punish and be done with it. Hurt a man physically, but don't, as incarceration does, destroy his life.

• • •

Along with a fondness for cricket and warm beer, the British exported the lash throughout their colonial empire (though we've moved on to baseball and cold beer). Although flogging is no longer on the books in any American state, it is still legal in thirty-three countries. But in nations where flogging is legal, at least if one judges by how often it is administered, only Singapore, Malaysia, and Brunei seem to thoroughly enjoy the process.

Both Amnesty International and the UN Human Rights Committee criticize flogging as cruel, degrading, and contrary to human rights law. Indeed, these organizations criticize all forms of corporal punishment. Yet the corporal-punishment holdouts seem to apply flogging with unrepentant zeal. Malaysia flogs perhaps 16,000 people a year. Singapore, with a population one-fifth of Malaysia, canes more than 6,000 a year. Singapore also has a very high incarceration rate of 267 per 100,000. Now, admittedly Singapore is a safe country, but if we're really looking for a role model, perhaps we should look at Japan, a country with low crime, no corporal punishment (though it does have the death penalty), and an incarceration rate one-fourth of Singapore's.

Recently I took the train to Singapore, from Thailand south through Malaysia, and I passed something of a landmark to caning. In 1976, at the border crossing leaving Thailand, Malaysian authorities caught Australian Robert Symes with four pounds of marijuana. Symes later said it was "fine grass" meant for himself and his stoner friends in Bali. But because it was such a large amount, Symes was convicted of drug trafficking. He narrowly escaped the death penalty and received prison plus six lashes. After being released, he described his caning in a magazine interview:

> The men responsible for administering this punishment know precisely what they are doing. They are pros. People about to be caned are given incredibly thorough medical checks before the punishment is administered—far more detailed checks than those given when a prisoner is admitted to a prison. If you die in prison from some ailment or other, too bad. But if you die from having your bum whacked, somebody somewhere is going to look bad.
>
> I was untied, and iodine was applied liberally to my wounds with a cotton swab. It stung like hell. . . .
>
> The cane had chewed hungrily through layers of skin and soft tissue, and had left furrows

that were . . . bloody pulp. The scars would never heal.

Perhaps the most famous case (at least in America) of modern flogging occurred in Singapore. Michael Fay was convicted in 1994 of spray-painting cars. (Fay admitted to stealing road signs but later claimed his vandalism confession was coerced.) After three months in jail, Fay received—and not by choice—four lashes. Although Fay's Singapore experience was not exceptionally different from what Symes went through in Malaysia, his story attracted massive attention in the United States because he was American, a teenager, and committed what here would barely be punished. After his caning, Fay appeared on *Larry King Live* and described his experience:

FAY: *The trestle, there was buckles on, for the feet, and there was buckles for the arms.*

KING: *Are you, like, prone?*

FAY: *Can I . . . can . . .*

KING: *Yeah, please.*

FAY: *I was bent over halfway. I mean, my back was bent, in a 90-degree [angle]. And I was buckled like this, so I couldn't get out of the buckle with my, my hands and my feet.*

KING: *Like a kid being spanked?*

FAY: *Exactly. . . . But much worse.*

KING: *Then what did they do? So you can't move your hands?*

FAY: *Right. You cannot move your hands or your feet. So you're stuck there. So, then the flogger . . . tested the cane a few times, to make sure. He would whip it. Yeah, whip it in the air. . . . He was actually in a T-shirt that said something like "Police Commandos." And he was wearing, like, army pants. . . . They yell out, "Count one." And he comes out and on the third step, and he's whipping, as he's going, on each step. And . . .*

KING: *Can you hear the whip?*

FAY: *Yes, you . . . yes, I can. And on the third, third step, he strikes. And he cuts open your buttocks.*

KING: *And there's a lot of pain?*

FAY: *There's a lot of pain.*

Fay's ordeal inspired strong reactions among Americans. In Dayton, Ohio, where Fay's father lived, a newspaper poll found two-to-one support for his punishment. Although many Americans were shocked at the thought of Fay being whipped, the fact is that he may have gotten off somewhat easy. Others have described far worse.

After his release, Fay returned to America and severely burnt himself while huffing butane. Because his family wasn't poor, he went into rehab. After a low-level drug arrest in 1998, he disappeared from the public's eye. Though he may still have the scars to remind him of his flogging, it seems as though the lash did not set Fay down a better path. But at least, it could be said, he never committed another act of vandalism in Singapore.

• • •

At this point the more open-minded reader may like pain as punishment but dislike the symbolism and messiness of flogging. Why not just build some kind of pain machine, push a button, and be done with it? A machine, perhaps much more than a person, could guarantee consistency of pain and also spare a person from having to administer the punishment.

Despite our best attempts—and yes, people have tried—a flogging machine is not a viable possibility. Disciplining machines are too ineffectual, too impersonal, and simply too bizarre to do the job. Consider this 1898 *New York Times* account of an "electric spanking chair" at a girls' school:

> It consists of a seatless chair on which the girls are placed. It is high enough from the ground to allow four paddles to be operated by electric wires. Straps hold the victim's wrists to the arm of the chair. . . . Bad girls are strapped in the chair, an attendant presses a button, and the chair does the rest. The Kansas authorities will be asked in a few days to explain this system.

Perhaps it wasn't painful enough, or perhaps girls could lift their butts just so, to avoid the paddles. Or perhaps the whole concept was just the silly invention of some perverted man. Regardless, the paper ran no further accounts of this chair.

But based on the description of the Kansas spanking chair, one could assume that punishment machines already exist in the worlds of bondage, S&M, or Russ Meyer films. Though I don't know from personal experience, I've seen some things online. Honestly, conducting any online research on flogging without stumbling across a wide variety of very adult websites is impossible. And I am naturally curious. But nothing (at least that doesn't require a credit card) matches the severity of the corporal punishment I defend. I propose something far beyond kink. If a flogging machine exists that can consistently and forcefully draw blood and still be less than lethal, I've yet to see it.

Flogging isn't the only way to cause pain. In *Just and Painful*, Graeme Newman's defense of corporal punishment, electric shock is the proposed method. Though Tasers were not around when Newman first wrote this excellent book, such "conducted energy devices" (as Tasers are generically known) could be an ideal way to give somebody an electric jolt. Many police departments use Tasers to gain compliance and subdue suspects. And although electric shock lacks the visual dramatics of flogging, Newman observes some advantages to using electric shock as corporal punishment: The severity of the punishment is easier to quantify, the process is nonscarring, and the administration of punishment is hands-off.

The problem with electric shocks, however, is that they sometimes kill. In the United States, police-administered Taser-like electric shock—and researchers are still catching up with this fact—kills more than one person per week, and that number is rising in sync with the increasingly widespread use of such devices. Sometimes a weak ticker is all it takes. In the other extreme, botched electrocutions show that people can live through terribly painful shocks. In truth we really don't know exactly how electricity affects the human body and brain, but we do know that lengthy or continued repetition of electric shock—the kind of application needed in a corporal punishment situation—greatly increases the risk of death.

Although perhaps some risk of death is acceptable when police on the street use the Taser as an alternative to lethal force (though many Tasers are used, somewhat worrisomely, in routine and non-threatening issues of noncompliance), there is no acceptable mortality rate in the administration of nonlethal sentences. Punishment, including corporal punishment, is explicitly *not* a death sentence. Whereas electric shocks sometimes kill without any visible warning, doctors could stop a flogging if a convict shows sign of strain, such as falling unconscious. If the doctor says the offender can't handle the lash, then it's back to jail for the offender. It may seem a bit absurd to have a doctor on hand to make certain a person is fit enough for a beating, but this is no different from a doctor's presence at a boxing match and is unquestionably a lot less absurd than a physical checkup before an execution.

Even if we could build an effective and nonlethal pain machine, leaving punishment in human hands would still be desirable. Machinelike consistency is not necessarily important. An expert trained in flogging and perhaps the martial arts would be best suited to punish, ensure the safety of the flogged, and stop before causing death. Furthermore, consecutive lashes should not be administered in exactly the same place: The goal is not to dredge a channel through an offender's body (as was depicted in Franz Kafka's short story "In the Penal Colony"). Instead, as is done in flogging cultures, the lashes are spread out across the entire flesh of the behind. This helps lower the risk of infection and keeps the pain from becoming beyond extreme. Nor does it matter if one flogger causes slightly more or less pain than another. Any such differences would pale in comparison with the variances already found at every other level of the American criminal justice system. (Although, because I hate to think of the licensing issues involved in training people to be official state floggers, I propose we poach expert floggers from Singapore and Malaysia, where it is a skilled and sought-after detail for law enforcement officers.)

There is another somewhat theoretical but perhaps more important argument against machine-administered punishment: Machines are *too* clean, too convenient. They psychologically sanitize what we are doing, allowing us to ignore the moral significance. If we can't face up to our form of punishing others, we shouldn't do it. If we want to punish, let's be honest about what we're doing. To do otherwise debases ourselves and, like prison, makes punishment an unhealthily removed and secretive concept. Consider Stanley Milgram's classic experiment on torture and authoritarian personalities: When ordered to by an authority figure, most people were willing to press a button and give what they believed to be an electric shock to another person. Although people generally have no desire to hurt those who have done nothing wrong, a button is too easy to press, a knob too easy to turn. The essential human element in physically causing pain helps us face and even limit the severity of whatever punishment we wish to administer. Pressing a button makes it too easy to torture.

Flogging is indeed very harsh, but it's not torture—not unless all corporal punishment is defined as torture. Indeed, to conflate flogging with torture does a grave disservice to the understanding of both. It is not only the physical act that defines torture but also the context, the psychological underpinnings, the lack of consent, and the open-ended potential. The US government has tortured people with euphemistically named "enhanced interrogation techniques." This torture is not so much a punishment as a means to an end. This is not flogging.

The distinction between pain as punishment and pain as torture is important. People torture because they're sadistic or want information. We punish because others have done wrong. The torture our government has sanctioned, which I in no way condone, was supposed to achieve a goal. Until that goal was achieved, torture continued. Punishment, however, is finite. It ends. Torture ends only when someone breaks. Punishment, unlike torture, is prescribed in accordance with clear rules of law. The difference between the goals and methods of punishment and torture is critical. I defend flogging, not torture.

Indeed, if examined closely, prisons much more so than flogging display characteristics of torture. By locking people in cells and denying meaningful human contact, we cause irreparable damage; by holding prisoners in group living quarters, we subject them to the potential of gang violence, assault, and all the other forms of aggression found in prisons; and through parole boards' decisions, we hold the power to continue such punishment for extended periods of time. And for what? What do we gain? Why incapacitate criminals in a nonrehabilitative environment never meant for punishment? This is more torturous than flogging could ever be.

Yes, flogging is nasty, brutish, and (blessedly) short. There's nothing pretty about it. Punishment is not supposed to be pretty. If it were, it wouldn't punish. And if punishment is necessary, we need to be honest about its horrific costs—and flogging is a much more humane (and economic) alternative.

Let me make an analogy about honesty in the infliction of pain. Think of meat. I don't think killing animals is good, but I like to eat meat. So when I do, I try to remember, even if briefly, that an animal lived and died for my sustenance (and pleasure). It's the least I can do. And although it's a convenience that I need not personally kill everything I eat, if I can't face up to the reality of animal death, then perhaps I shouldn't eat meat. Think of it the next time you go to the grocery store. A lot has happened between a cow's moo and a shrink-wrapped steak.

If you are brave, there are ways to confront the true cost of eating meat. You can hunt or, more feasible in the big city, at least see your dinner alive before you eat it. And I'm not just talking about lobster tanks. There are two live-poultry stores near me, and one even has a little "pasture" out back filled with lambs and sometimes the occasional cow. I call it the "petting zoo" because when I'm there that's what I like to do. If I want to roast one of the lambs, I can point to one and have it dragged out of the pen to be killed, skinned, cleaned, and cut. Is it pretty? Well, not really. But at least it's honest. And if you eat meat, this process is inevitable whether you close your eyes to it or not. Muffling the sounds of suffering in the world is one thing— after all, if we didn't, we would all go crazy—but pretending suffering doesn't exist is quite another.

Flogging is refreshingly transparent and honest. What you see is what you get. If you want someone to receive more punishment, you give more lashes. If you want them to receive less punishment, you give fewer. Prison, however, is dishonest punishment. We on the outside have no real idea what goes on inside the concertina wire, but let's not fool ourselves: It's bleak. Prisons and slaughterhouses are two of the very few institutions closed to visitors. Just as we prefer not to know all the details of how meat ends up on our table, we prefer to keep prisoners out of sight and mind. Bad things tend to happen in secret, when the masses of "decent" folks can't or don't want to see what happens to others.

Just as we want to eat meat without thinking of slaughter, we want to punish without thinking of pain. But you cannot have one without the other. There is a very real damage in the way we choose to punish criminals, and we need to face this instead of pretending it doesn't happen. The treatment of living, sentient beings matters. And presumably, I hope, people care more about the treatment of a human than a cow. Indeed, our criminal justice system has become a bit too much like Soylent Green, the basic foodstuff from the 1973 movie set in the dystopian future of 2022. In *Soylent Green*, it turns out that corporately produced Soylent Green is—spoiler alert—"*made of people!*" So is our system of corrections.

. . .

Even as flogging is more open and honest than prison, this may not persuade some critics, so the fact that flogging is cheap—much less expensive than prison—is worth some elaboration. The financial argument is extremely important and also straightforward. Leaving aside everything already mentioned about the horrors of prison, incarceration simply costs too much (especially considering how ineffective it is). Although there is a fixed cost in establishing any system of judicial punishment—the courts, lawyers, jails, appeals, and police officers—compared to a system of incarceration, the actual cost of flogging is miniscule.

Criminal justice—considering how abjectly it fails at the goals we've set out for it—is ludicrously expensive. Take, for example, just two criminal families in Birmingham, England (but the results would likely be similar in the United States). Over three generations of police investigations, lawyers, trials, and prison for serious crimes, these two families cost taxpayers £37 million (about $59 million). The total cost of the larger gangs of which these two families were a part—and this is a conservative estimate that does not include medical care for victims, minor crimes, or welfare and housing benefits the families claimed—was close to a staggering £190 million ($300 million). This is not money well spent. As one politician put it, "We spend vast sums of money ineffectually managing social failure."

Prisons are expensive not because they coddle prisoners—quite the opposite; prisons cost so much because we have to keep people alive while holding them against their will. It's not an easy task. Prisoners require human observation and intervention, and it's not a nine-to-five operation; rather, officers have to be present day and night to maintain order and guard the prisoners. To have one guard on duty 24/7 requires *six* employees (taking into account three shifts, weekends, and holidays). Conversely, flogging requires but a trestle on which to flog, a few law enforcement officers, a doctor, and the actual flogger. With the exception of the flogger and the furniture, everything is already in place. Compared to prison, flogging is essentially free.

A quick look at the numbers shows just how much could be saved by abandoning incarceration. Estimates put corrections spending at somewhere between $60 billion and $78 billion per year. Either amount could safely be called "real money." The actual savings would vary greatly, from a low of $13,000 per prisoner per a year in Louisiana to $70,000 in New York City. Nationwide, on average, it costs $26,000 for each year of incarceration. This means that each additional year of prison costs another $26,000. But an additional lash is free.

If we could drastically reduce incarceration, the greatest question may be what to do with all the money. Might it not be more effective to give the money we currently spend on keeping offenders locked up to help those in need? What we spend on prison could be used to help people and to prevent crime. I have a friend, a former student, who had a rough childhood. He was the first in his family to graduate from college. Nevertheless, he's recently unemployed and trying to support his family on something other than the drug dealing he grew up with. When I told him the financial cost of prison, he said, "*How much?* Man, the government never spent that kind of money on me growing up.

Why not just give me that money and I'll stay straight. I'd stay straight for half that!"

Even if, given our current levels of recidivism, it might be a good investment to give money to people to stay out of crime, politically and also morally, it's a tough sell. More palatable might be to give money to victims of crime. Crime victims suffer trauma, medical bills, and lost wages, but we can't fine the typical criminal because he's broke. I know giving money to crime victims isn't completely realistic; two obvious problems would be desperate people faking crimes and money going to some rather unsavory "victims"—after all, a crime victim is often just a criminal having a bad day. But some of the money saved by flogging should be used to help real victims.

Imagine once again being the victim of a violent mugging. The mugger is convicted and sentenced to five years in prison or ten lashes. He, as expected, chooses the lash. You might feel better knowing the offender will be caned, but that doesn't assuage the financial and emotional costs you've borne. As soon as the mugger consents to be flogged, and here's a new concept, the judge could turn to you to either accept the criminal's decision or reject it and send him to prison. The victim could receive money if the criminal is flogged. For every two lashes the prisoner receives, thus knocking a year off the sentence, the crime victim could receive $13,000. You, the victim, can choose for the criminal to receive anywhere from zero to ten lashes, with any remaining sentence being served in prison. In essence, the state will split the money saved by not incarcerating. You win, the taxpayer wins, even the criminal wins. Where's the harm? Taking account of victims' concerns as a means of diverting people from jail generally falls under the rubric of "restorative justice," yet it is unlikely that advocates of restorative justice will support my defense of flogging.

...

I've already mentioned some of flogging's basic rules throughout the preceding pages: Immediacy, proportionality, transparency, and choice are all critical components in a just system of corporal punishment. And though a philosophical defense of flogging shouldn't get bogged down in nitty-gritty details, I would be remiss not to discuss in greater detail how, exactly, flogging would work. Here, then, are some basic guidelines for implementing flogging in a civilized and even progressive society:

- Flogging can only be done with the consent of the flogged. The status quo of incarceration is always an option.
- Immediately upon arrest, suspects should be classified as to whether they're imminent and grave dangers to society. Some offenders do need to be incarcerated and kept away from society. But for the vast majority of criminal suspects, flogging would be a viable option.
- Misdemeanants could opt, as a plea bargain, to be flogged immediately and released, before any court decision.
- Just as today (but this would be much quicker), prosecutors would offer felons a plea deal based on the severity of their crime.
- Incarceration should be converted to lashes using a formula of two lashes per year. For shorter sentences, one stroke could be the acceptable minimum punishment for a misdemeanor and two for a felony. For the safety of the flogged, thirty strokes would be the prescribed maximum, though

this number could vary depending on the advice of a doctor.

- Flogging is an alternative to incarceration, not an addition to it. The purpose of flogging is to punish and be done with it.

- The cane itself, as used in Singapore, is a rattan piece approximately four feet long and half an inch thick. Before use, the cane is soaked in water to add weight and flexibility and is treated with antiseptic.

- Only a person trained in the use of the lash can administer the caning, and it must be done on a person's behind. A doctor must be present. Any scars left from the lash should not be immediately visible to others. Just as punishments should not be a permanent source of shame, they should also, one would hope, not be a lasting source of pride.

- Floggings should take place in one session and be administered as soon as possible after the consent of the flogged. The punished should be released immediately after the punishment and any needed medical care.

In large cities one caning trestle should be in the courthouse and another in Central Booking so that those arrested on misdemeanors could immediately assent to being flogged. After an arrest or conviction, one could accept a flogging plea and go to the caning room. This punishment would not serve as the basis for public gatherings or celebrations. This area would be open to the public but not have unrestricted public access. A nontelevised courtroom setting is an appropriate model. As in a courtroom, proper decorum would be enforced.

The person to be flogged would be inspected by a doctor, tied to a whipping post, and stripped at the butt. The flogger would enter the room, perform a few warm-up snaps of the cane, and then commence. After the proper number of lashes, the offender would again be examined by a doctor, have any wounds tended to, and be sent on his or her way. The punishment would be complete after only a few minutes of brutal pain.

. . .

When I defend flogging, and perhaps I shouldn't be surprised, I sometimes get strange looks. Some friends have been known to question my sincerity and others my sanity. Too often, they just don't get it. One colleague begged me to reconsider for the sake of my professional career (I hope she's wrong). But also worrisome is when people say, "Great idea! Right on!" The need for flogging is not something that should be celebrated. I have no intention or desire to glorify caning. On the contrary, I hope never to see it. And yet I firmly believe flogging is better than what we have, both for society and for those being punished.

Flogging is not a slippery step toward amputation, public stoning, or sharia law. This is not the first step on a path to hell. A lesser society might go down this road by *imposing* flogging on its citizens and then descending into mob rule and blood sport. But we are a stable democracy with a longstanding tradition of deference to the rule of law. As an alternative to prison, the option of flogging does not mark a shift toward some barbaric dark age.

Quite the contrary. For those who suffer under the yoke of incarceration, for the millions of Americans behind bars, the age already is dark. Indeed, we would be deeply deluded—if not downright duplicitous—to express horror at the violence inherent in legal judicial flogging and, by doing so, condone the much more insidious violence inherent in jail and prison. Opposition to flogging often seems to come not from a desire to protect the person being flogged but from a more selfish desire to protect the punisher.

Differences in political opinion should make little difference when considering flogging as an acceptable substitute for prison. If you're conservative, flogging holds appeal as efficient, cheap, and old-fashioned punishment for wrongdoing. It's a "get tough" approach too; at least symbolically, nothing is tougher than the lash. If you're liberal and your goal is to punish more effectively and humanely, then you first must accept that the present system is an inhumane failure. Do not seek minor improvements to our prison system; think instead of massive replacements. Prisons can be improved, but they cannot be reformed. The best prison in the world is still a prison. And an institution whose purpose is forced detention will forever and inevitably remain dysfunctional. Our responsibility as men and women of conscience is to find a functional solution—and flogging may well be it. Let the person being punished decide.

Maybe by this point you're convinced that flogging is a viable alternative, but you still don't feel comfortable with the lash. You're confused because you agree that the case for flogging is a sound one, but deep down you still know that flogging is wrong. You know what? I agree. Other things being equal, I don't want to live with flogging, either. But we have to face the world we live in. If the mere thought of purposefully inflicting pain offends your sensibilities, consider how Charles Dickens summoned up his own moral courage after witnessing the effects of solitary life in a prison cell:

> I hesitated once, debating with myself, whether, if I had the power of saying "Yes" or "No," I would allow it to be tried in certain cases, where the terms of imprisonment were short; but now, I solemnly declare, that with no rewards or honours could I walk a happy man beneath the open sky by day, or lie me down upon my bed at night, with the consciousness that one human creature, for any length of time, no matter what, lay suffering this unknown punishment in his silent cell, and I the cause, or I consenting to it in the least degree.

Since his day, prison has not gotten better; we have gotten worse. And since Dickens's time we still have not devised a better way to punish. Without an alternative such as flogging, we all consent to the horrors Dickens describes.

With the invention of prisons, confident penology experts could boast (and perhaps even believe) that the massive fortifications of the prison wall were modern displays of science and technology. The move away from punishment toward cure was indeed a monumental change, a genuine (if misguided) moral and scientific revolution. But truthfully, I can't think of another institution that has failed as mightily as the prison has—at each and every one of its initial objectives—and then, over the course of two hundred years, expanded and been rewarded with ever-increasing civic and political power.

To not debate the effectiveness of prison would be like accepting a health care system that diagnosed illnesses with phrenology (the "science" of determining character through skull shape) and treated them with Wilhelm Reich's orgone accumulators (something even crazier). The fact that prisons have so completely failed—and done so in such a spectacular manner—should matter more than it does.

Flogging could restore legitimacy to a criminal justice system that is in desperate need of it. Since flogging's demise, have we as a society really progressed? Or did we take the noble but flawed ideal of criminal rehabilitation and distort it into a perverse system of almost unimaginable cruelty? The lash, which metes out punishment without falsely promising betterment, is an unequivocal expression of society's condemnation. For those flogged, it is brief, painful, and very easy to comprehend.

Without a radical defense of flogging, how else are we to change our current defective system of justice? Reformers laud bits of incremental improvement that come at a glacial pace. But, at best, these only tinker with the massive machinery of incarceration. Bringing back the lash is one way to destroy it—if not completely, then at least for the millions of Americans for whom the punishment of prison is far, far worse than the crime they have committed.

Years from now, if we're lucky, future generations will look back to this age of mass incarceration with bemused wonder, seeing it as just another unfortunate blotch on our country's otherwise noble democratic ideals. Either that or they will judge us as willing collaborators in an unparalleled atrocity of human bondage. Let us hope for the former, but future moral condemnation is all but assured; consider the three predictive factors listed by Princeton philosophy professor Kwame Anthony Appiah. First, the case against the institution is long established and doesn't "emerge in a blinding moment of moral clarity." Certainly, though my defense of flogging may be novel, people have long taken moral stands against prisons. Second, according to Appiah, defenders tend to invoke tradition, human nature, or necessity rather than moral arguments, which are essentially ceded to opponents. Today, prison's biggest supporters emphasize the necessity of jobs and economic development. Finally, supporters tend to practice "strategic ignorance, avoiding truths that might force them to face the evils in which they're complicit." Today, nobody but the most naive person argues that prisons are good for prisoners or that solitary confinement is a path toward spiritual salvation. And yet still people fool themselves with talk of country-club prisons and "three hots and a cot." This somehow implies that because prisons could actually be worse, then somehow they must be good.

People will look back to our age of incarceration and, thinking of us, ask: "Did they not know? Did they not care?" We must find a replacement, and flogging, however harsh, is one such alternative. Over the past two centuries we somehow decided that flogging is beneath us in much the same arbitrary and mistaken way we determined prisons are good. That Americans will someday have to reckon with the immorality of mass incarceration seems abundantly clear. Let us pray the judge of history is lenient. If not, I hate to think of how we would be punished.

· · ·

In a short book like this, I have inevitably had to gloss over some of the issues related to flogging: the moral qualms, the spattered blood, lawsuits, policy details, and a certain retrograde feeling to the whole proposition. I've allowed myself to do so because, at the end of the day, these details are less important than the larger theme. My intention is to open your eyes to our massive and horrible system of incarceration. I am willing to defend flogging to start an honest discussion on punishment and alternatives to prison. I've tried to convince you to accept flogging, but I've done so in order to convince you that the status quo of incarceration is much, much worse. If you feel half-convinced and slightly queasy, well, good. That was my goal.

Please do not close this book thinking once again that somehow things really aren't that bad or that prison is just the way it has to be. Prisons continue to perpetuate crime, drain our wallets, and cause untold human suffering because we—good people, people of conscience—do nothing. Tomorrow, 2.3 million Americans—mothers, fathers, sons, and daughters—will wake up behind bars. If one person behind bars is tragic, are 2.3 million simply a statistic? Many have done some very bad things, but each one is still a human being. Do we leave them to rot in prison because we cannot bear to confront the necessary reality of punishment? Are Americans so evil that we must confine more of our own people than every other nation in the world?

I hope you can see that we need to find a new way to punish, an option that won't subject offenders and society to this expensive and immoral failure. If flogging is that option, well, then bring on the lash.

ACKNOWLEDGMENTS

Writing a book can be quite lonely, but it is never solitary. This book would never have been written were it not for the ideas and help of others. Dan Baum and Margaret Knox planted the seed for *In Defense of Flogging* over dinner in New Orleans in 2007—the first of many such dinners, I'm happy to say—when the conversation turned to parental support for illegal corporal punishment in public schools. When I mentioned this phrase to Tim Sullivan, my editor at the time, he informed me in no uncertain terms that he was going to publish a book by that name, I was going to write it, and there would be no question mark in the title.

In the subsequent years, many others have helped tremendously. In particular I thank Lara Heimert and Alex Littlefield at Basic Books, who took on this project and managed, in very short time, to whip chaos into something approaching a proper book.

Maurice Punch helped with his inspiration and curry dinners; Graeme Newman defended corporal punishment long before I ever thought of the idea, and did so far more persuasively than I ever will. Mitch Duneier, as always, has been incredibly supportive (to me and seemingly everybody who has ever crossed his path). C. Farrell helped immeasurably with his personal assistance and encyclopedic (and sane) corporal-punishment website. Jennifer Wynn hated this idea from day one and yet, because it is her nature, couldn't help but be supportive and helpful. Andrew Moskos, my brother, always thinks of funny things to say. And special thanks to my mother, Ilca Moskos, who isn't afraid to tell me when my writing "isn't quite there yet." (Strangely, and despite my memories to the contrary, she claims never to have spanked me.)

Thanks also to all those who gave me ideas and comments, engaged me in conversation, and helped me get tenure: Elijah Anderson, Howard Becker, Rod Ben Zeev, Joel and Kaori Busch, Lawrence Campbell, Effie Papatzkou Cochran, Jane De Lung, Brandon del Pozo, Gary Alan Fine, Neill Franklin, Lior Gideon, Jim Greer, Maki Haberfeld, Jennifer Hunt, Maurice Jacobs, Daphne Keller, Harry Levine, Jim and Masha Lidbury, Patty Jean Lidbury, John Van Maanen, Saskia Maas, Peter Manning, Timothy Manrow, Gloria Marshall, Jeff Mellow, Jaqueline Nieves, Zoë Pagnamenta, Orlando Patterson, Jackie Pica, Joseph Pollini, Karine Schaefer, Dorothy Schulz, Wesley Skogan, Barry Spunt, Howard Taylor, Katie Trainor, Leon Vainikos, Melissa Veronesi, Charles Westoff, Chris Winship, the St. Nicolaas Boat Club of Amsterdam, and all my colleagues and students at John Jay College of Criminal Justice, LaGuardia Community College, and the City University of New York's Sociology Graduate Center.

And finally, to twist a phrase a friend once told me: "Don't marry for copy-editing skills; hang around copy editors and fall in love." So special thanks to Zora O'Neill and her eagle eye.

NOTES

1   *whipping, caning, lashing, call it what you will*: Technically, what I propose is caning and not whipping: A whip is made of flexible leather, whereas the cane is a more rigid stick; a whip is snapped and cracked, but a cane is simply swung with great force. Both whipping and caning fall under the more general category of flogging. But the differences between whipping and caning are all but irrelevant to my defense of flogging (though the whip does have more troubling racial symbolism in the United States). For all practical purposes, the concepts of whipping and caning can be considered one and the same.

3   *jail for almost anything, big or small*: Harvey A. Silverglate, *Three Felonies a Day: How the Feds Target the Innocent* (New York: Encounter Books, 2009). The author estimates that most Americans unknowingly commit three felonies a day with enforcement simply subject to the whims of prosecutorial discretion.

5   *a "total institution" of complete dominance and regulation*: Erving Goffman, *Asylums: Essays on the Social Situation of Mental Patients and Other Inmates* (New York: Penguin, 1968). Michel Foucault would later combine Goffman's concept of total institution with Bentham's Panopticon to create his classic *Discipline and Punish*. Not completely by accident, I give Foucault short shrift in this book. Considering Foucault's

mighty influence in the philosophy of punishment, one could, if one were so inclined, add some variation of "as Foucault alludes to" to the beginning of almost every paragraph; I am not so inclined. With no disrespect to hundreds of graduate-student seminars and dissertations, I think Foucault is overrated. In what is considered academic sacrilege, I do not like Foucault. Mostly I dislike his style of writing (though this might be a problem of translation, as I do not speak the original French). Too often Foucault disguises rather simple concepts in verbosity and awkward prose. I believe *Discipline and Punish* can be well summarized in nothing more than two simple seventeen-syllable haikus:

society's norms—more like prisons every day—
resistance is futile

from body to mind—a new system of control—
the Panopticon

Were I to include a more thorough heady discussion of French philosophy littered with casual allusions to Foucault, it would be nothing more than academic pretension.

10   *I'm starting to dream about the prison*: Ken Lewis and Aaron Cohen, "Horror of the Lash: 500 Lashes a Death Sentence," *New Zealand Truth & TV Extra*, October 10, 1997, cited at World Corporal Punishment Research, www.corpun.com/myju9710.htm.

12   *antiseptic on the caning wound*: P. M. Raman, "Branding the Bad Hats for Life," *Singapore Straits Times*, September 13, 1974, www.corpun.com/sgju7409.htm.

14   *prisoners outnumbers the US Marines*: "How Many Corrections Officers Are There?" Corrections Community, http://community.nicic.org/forums/p/5894/11704.aspx.

15   *we incarcerated 338,000 people*: Justice Policy Institute, "The Punishing Decade: Prison and Jail Estimates at the Millennium," May 2000, www.justicepolicy.org/images/upload/00–05_REP_PunishingDecade_AC.pdf.

15   *"only a shocking level of failure"*: National Advisory Commission on Criminal Justice Standards and Goals, *Task Force Report on Corrections* (Washington, DC: Government Printing Office, 1973), 358, 597.

17   *may very well have bankrupted the state*: Frank Zimring, "The Decline in Crime in New York City," Vera Institute of Justice, 2010, www.vera.org/videos/franklin-zimring-decline-crime-new-york-city. For comparison, the budget of the New York City Police Department is $4.4 billion.

17   *foreign immigrants moved to New York City*: *The Newest New Yorkers 2000: Immigrant New York in the New Millennium* (New York: New York City Department of City Planning, Population Division, 2004), 8, 10.

23   *death penalty still runs three to one*: Unpublished data graciously provided by Angus Reid Public Opinion, December 2010. Support for the death penalty among those who believe the death penalty does not deter crime is 73 percent. For related data, see *Americans Support Punishing Murder with the Death Penalty*, Angus Reid Public Opinion, November 9, 2010.

25   *prison ships docked in New York City*: Edwin G. Burrows, *Forgotten Patriots: The Untold Story of American Prisoners During the Revolutionary War* (New York: Basic Books, 2010).

26   *"cannot possibly make their escape"*: Richard H. Phelps, *Newgate of Connecticut; Its Origin and Early History* (Hartford, CT: American Publishing Company, 1876), 53.

30   *more conducive to salvation and healing*: Thorsten Sellin, "The House of Correction for Boys in the Hospice of Saint Michael in Rome," *Journal of the American Institute of Criminal Law and Criminology* 20, no. 4 (February 1930): 533–53. The idea of solitary confinement likely came to Howard after he visited the Saint Michael's House of Correction for Boys in Rome. Founded in 1704 at the request of the pope, this institution appears to be the first to enforce solitary confinement.

31   *be far more effective than flogging*: Negley K. Teeters, *The Cradle of the Penitentiary: The Walnut Street Jail at Philadelphia, 1773–1835* (Philadelphia: Pennsylvania Prison Society, 1955), 32.

32   *"a simple idea in Architecture!"*: Jeremy Bentham, *Panopticon*
        (Dublin: T. Payne, 1791), i–ii. Bentham's lengthy subtitle
        reveals the scope and potential application for his system for
        total surveillance and control: *or the Inspection-House: Con-*
        taining the idea of a new principle of construction applicable
        to any sort of establishment, in which persons of any description
        are to be kept under inspection; and in particular to penitentiary-
        houses, prisons, houses of industry, work-houses, poor-houses,
        lazarettos, manufactories, hospitals, mad-houses, and schools:
        with a plan of management adapted to the principle. Much of
        this, as (ahem) Foucault would be quick to point out, has
        become commonplace today with such things as ubiquitous
        surveillance cameras. Though what Bentham could not know
        and Foucault failed to see is that, short of solitary confine-
        ment, there can be no complete and effective system of
        total control.

33   *isolation, monitoring, and "apparent omnipresence"*: Ibid., 28.

34   *"by small measure, by the gaoler."*: Teeters, *The Cradle of the*
        Penitentiary, 132.

34   *long Washington's political adversary*: In 1787 Procter hosted
        a going-away dinner for George Washington. The bill lists
        massive amounts of alcohol, more than two bottles of wine
        per person in addition to substantial quantities of "old stock,"
        beer, hard cider, and alcoholic punch. Each servant and mu-
        sician received a bottle of wine in addition to pay.

34–35   *15 of whom succeeded*: James Mease, *Picture of Philadelphia*
        (Philadelphia: B. & T. Kite, 1811), 164.

35   *for only a third of those admitted*: Rex A. Skidmore, "Peno-
        logical Pioneering in the Walnut Street Jail, 1789–1799,"
        Journal of Criminal Law & Criminology 39, no. 2 (July/
        August 1948), 167–80.

35   *that from a* sympathetic *account*: Mease, *Picture of Philadel-*
        phia, 166.

35   *resolved issues of racially based gangs*: *Johnson v. California*,
        543 U.S. 499 (2005); Don Thompson, "California Struggles
        To Desegregate Inmates," *San Francisco Chronicle*, August
        13, 2009.

36   *the very nature of the being is changed*: Mease, *Picture of Philadelphia*, 168. That one of the first prison wardens, Mary Weed, was a woman, is noteworthy. She took over after her husband died of yellow fever in 1793, held the paid position of "principle keeper" for three years, and left on good terms in 1796.

37   *"one to take care of the other."*: Edwin G. Burrows and Mike Wallace, *Gotham: A History of New York City to 1898* (New York: Oxford, 1998), 366.

37   *Newgate Prison in Greenwich Village*: Ibid. Early prisons were often named Newgate after the notorious centuries-old jail in London. This scare tactic, prison commissioners hoped, would serve to deter crime a bit more.

37   *"and a popular form of government."*: Ibid.

37   *was also clearly punishment*: Ibid., 367.

38   *believe reformers' curative promises*: Mark Colvin, *Penitentiaries, Reformatories, and Chain Gangs: Social Theory and the History of Punishment in Nineteenth-Century America* (New York: St. Martin's Press, 1997), 56.

38   *"the bitter pangs of remorse."*: Burrows and Wallace, *Gotham*, 366–67.

38   *"the arts and practices of criminality."*: Ibid., 505–506.

38   *incarceration was driving people insane*: Atul Gawande, "Hellhole: The United States holds tens of thousands of inmates in long-term solitary confinement. Is this torture?" *New Yorker*, March 30, 2009, www.newyorker.com/reporting/2009/03/30/090330fa_fact_gawande.

38   *to prevent prisoners from escaping*: Burrows and Wallace, *Gotham*, 367.

39   *upriver Sing Sing in 1826*: Ibid., 367. Almost two hundred years later, both Auburn and Sing Sing are still in operation.

40   *"fixed provision made for this purpose."*: Bentham, *Panopticon*, 10–11.

41   *found here together with the prisoners*: Gustave de Beaumont and Alexis de Tocqueville, *On the Penitentiary System in the United States and Its Application in France*, translated by Francis Lieber (Philadelphia: Carey, Lea & Blanchard, 1833), 13.

41   *"that Auburn is "next preferable.":* Ibid., 60, 46, xi.

42   *"wise advice and pious exhortation.":* Ibid., 5, 51.

42   *"moral power" of silence and labor:* Ibid., ix.

43   *"agony . . . upon his fellow-creature.":* Charles Dickens, "Chapter VII: Philadelphia, and Its Solitary Prison," in *American Notes for General Circulation and Pictures from Italy* (London: Chapman and Hall, 1874), 114–15.

44   *ordered Medley, a convicted killer, freed:* Medley, 134 U.S. 160 (1890). Unfortunately, there is no account of how Medley fared with his second chance in life. In its decision the court was well aware that many prisoners in solitary committed suicide, and "a considerable number of the prisoners fell, after even a short confinement, into a semi-fatuous condition, from which it was next to impossible to arouse them, and others became violently insane." Those who survived were generally not reformed and, in most cases, "did not recover sufficient mental activity to be of any subsequent service to the community."

46   *imprisonment as a means of promoting rehabilitation:* Mistretta v. United States, 488 U.S. 361 (1989).

47   *"an informant on other prisoners.":* Alexander Cockburn, "Going Insane in the SHU Box," *Los Angeles Times,* July 15, 2001.

48   *novel idea to deliberately fill the state's jails:* Robert Martinson, "Prison Notes of a Freedom Rider," *The Nation,* January 6, 1962. Martinson's group of Freedom Riders was arrested for integrating the "white" waiting room of the Jackson, Mississippi, train station. The governor decided to move the Freedom Riders from local jail to the Parchmann State Penitentiary. As a result, Martinson spent time in maximum security solitary confinement. Martinson, who remained unbroken by his brief time in prison, wrote, "It is impossible to prepare anyone for the humiliating, brutal atmosphere of even the best prison. There are no rules, no precedents."

48   *known in policy circles as "Nothing Works!":* Robert Martinson, "What Works? Questions and Answers About Prison Reform," *The Public Interest* 35 (Spring 1974), 22–54.

49   *"heart of the matter better than I did."*: Robert Martinson, "New Findings, New Views: A Note of Caution Regarding Sentencing," *Hofstra Law Review* 7 (1979): 243–58.

49   *by jumping out a Manhattan window*: Jerome G. Miller, "Criminology: Is Rehabilitation a Waste of Time?" *Washington Post*, April 23, 1989, C3. Sasha Abramsky, *American Furies: Crime, Punishment, and Vengeance in the Age of Mass Imprisonment* (Boston: Beacon Press, 2007), 53.

50   *kick the ball-encased person down a field*: An elephant ball is on display at the Corrections Museum in Bangkok, Thailand.

50–51 *"ever fallen to the lot of mere mortality."*: Edgar Allan Poe, *The Complete Tales and Poems of Edgar Allan Poe* (New York: Random House, 1975), 258.

51   *"literally buried from the world."*: Roger T. Pray, "How Did Our Prisons Get That Way?" *American Heritage Magazine* 38, no. 5 (1987), www.americanheritage.com/articles/magazine/ah/1987/5/1987_5_92.shtml.

51   *for about eight years now*: From the Crime Report, cited as originally appearing in "A Letter To No One" in *The Beat Within*, http://thecrimereport.org/2010/10/31/the-beat-within-a-letter-to-no-one.

52   *assaulted by other inmates or staff in the past year*: Allen J. Beck, Paige M. Harrison, Marcus Berzofsky, Rachel Caspar, and Christopher Krebs, "Sexual Victimization in Prisons and Jails Reported by Inmates, 2008–09" (Washington, DC: US Department of Justice, 2010).

53   *and his life is in further danger*: Edward Charles, "Prison 101: What you need to know before you go to prison," 2010, www.wild-side.com/darksorrow/prison101.html.

55   *the wrong spot and the wrong time*: "The Prisoners of the War on Drugs," HBO, 1996.

55   *BAM! Prison*: www.99chan.in/b, downloaded October 18, 2010.

56   *guys like me is inside the penitentiary*: "The Prisoners of the War on Drugs."

57   *"to get you some money down here."*: Ibid.

58   *half of whom have multiple prior convictions*: Thomas H. Cohen and Tracey Kyckelhahn, "Felony Defendants in Large Urban Counties, 2006," Office of Justice Programs, Bureau of Justice Statistics, May 2010, http://bjs.ojp.usdoj.gov/content/pub/pdf/fdluc06.pdf. The nation's seventy-five largest counties cover about 35 percent of America's population.

58   *even years before their day in court*: Lise Olsen, "Thousands Languish in Crowded Jail: Inmates Can Stay Locked Up More Than a Year Waiting for Trial in Low-level Crimes," *Houston Chronicle*, August 23, 2009.

59   *16,500 did not post bail*: Mosi Secret, "N.Y.C. Misdemeanor Defendants Lack Bail Money," *New York Times*, December 2, 2010.

60   *could receive even if found guilty*: Olsen, "Thousands Languish in Crowded Jail."

62   *adrenaline and the thrill of the crime*: Jack Katz, *Seductions of Crime* (New York: Basic Books, 1988).

62   *similar criminals who don't go to prison*: C. Spohn and D. Holleran, "The Effect of Imprisonment on Recidivism Rates of Felony Offenders: A Focus on Drug Offenders," *Criminology* 40 (2002), 329–58; Joan Petersilia and Susan Turner, "Prison Versus Probation in California: Implications for Crime and Offender Recidivism" (Santa Monica, CA: RAND, 1986).

63   *into self-sufficient criminal creators*: Martin H. Pritikin, "Is Prison Increasing Crime?" *Wisconsin Law Review*, no. 6 (2008), 1049.

63   *high school diploma do time in prison*: Bruce Western, *Punishment and Inequality in America* (New York: Russell Sage Foundation, 2006).

69   *as high as the white poverty rate*: In 2009 the US Census defined poverty in the United States as an individual making less than $11,161, a couple $14,439, and a family of four $21,756. At $7.25 an hour, a full-time minimum wage job pays $15,080 a year.

70   *arrested for marijuana possession*: See the work of Harry Levine of Queens College, including Harry G. Levine, Jon B. Gettman, and Loren Siegel, *Arresting Blacks for Marijuana*

in California Possession Arrests in 25 Cities, 2006–08, Drug Policy Alliance, 2010.

72   *One in five Americans was a slave*: 18 percent, according to the 1790 census.

74   *because of a past felony conviction*: Figures range from 827,000 to 960,000. The former is from Jeff Manza and Christopher Uggen's *Locked Out: Felon Disenfranchisement and American Democracy* (New York: Oxford University Press, 2006). The latter is from "Felony Disenfranchisement Laws in the United States," The Sentencing Project, 2010, www.sentencing project.org/doc/publications/fd_bs_fdlawsinusMarch2010 .pdf.

74   *5.3 million Americans are denied the vote*: "Felony Disenfranchisement Laws in the United States."

74   *"They don't vote, so, I guess, not really."*: Sam Roberts, "Census Bureau's Counting of Prisoners Benefits Some Rural Voting Districts," *New York Times*, October 23, 2008, www.ny times.com/2008/10/24/us/politics/24census.html?_r=1.

74   *slavery, to segregation, to incarceration*: Loïc Wacquant, *Punishing the Poor: The Neoliberal Government of Social Insecurity* (Durham, NC: Duke University Press, 2009).

77   *the business of incarceration*: Peter Wagner, *The Prison Index: Taking the Pulse of the Crime Control Industry* (Northampton, MA: The Prison Policy Initiative, 2003). To give but one example, the market to control collect calls from prisoners is $1 billion per year. Collect calls from jail and prison can cost dollars per minute. Part of the phone company's profit is then kicked back to the state or county in the form of a highest-bidder contract to provide phone service.

77   *by building housing for the poor*: Eric Schlosser, "The Prison-Industrial Complex," *The Atlantic*, December 1998. The term itself was coined by Mike Davis in "Hell Factories in the Field: The Prison Industrial Complex," *Nation*, February 20, 1995.

78   *literally and figuratively left and right*: Ben Carrasco and Joan Petersilia, "Assessing the CCPOA's Political Influence and Its Impact on Efforts to Reform the California Corrections System," California Sentencing & Corrections Policy Series,

Stanford Criminal Justice Center Working Papers, www.law
.stanford.edu/program/centers/scjc/workingpapers/BCarassco
-wp4_06.pdf.

78   *correctional officer is a difficult job*: Ted Conover, *Newjack:
Guarding Sing Sing* (New York: Riverhead, 2004). Conover
worked as a correctional officer in Sing Sing, and *Newjack* is probably the best single account of a very difficult
occupation.

79   *to prosecute a guard for assault*: Stephen James, "Decline of
the Empire," *Sacramento News & Review* (March 17, 2005).

80   *roughly the same level as unionized prison guards*: *Occupational
Outlook Handbook, 2010–11 Edition, Correctional Officers*
(Washington, DC: Bureau of Labor Statistics, 2009), www
.bls.gov/oco/ocos156.htm; Corrections Corporation of
America, "CAA Announces Fourth Quarter and Full-Year
2009 Financial Results," press release, February 9, 2010,
http://ir.correctionscorp.com/phoenix.zhtml?c=117983&p=
irol-newsArticle&id=1385706. There is no reason to single
out the Corrections Corporation of America. They are not
the worst of the private prison companies, only the largest.
In 2008 median annual wages for correctional officers in the
public sector were $50,830 for the federal government,
$38,850 for state government, and $37,510 for local government. For private prisons, median wages are $28,790.

80   *turnover rate of 40 percent annually*: Wagner, *The Prison Index*.
The comparable rate for the public sector is 15 percent.

81   *"If we build it, they will come."*: Robert B. Gunnison, "Pri-
vately Run Prison Planned for Mojave," *San Francisco Chronicle*, August 1, 1997.

81   *country illegally who were facing deportation*: Joseph T. Hal-
linan, "Federal Government Saves Private Prisons as State
Convict Population Levels Off," *Wall Street Journal*, November 6, 2001.

81   *town residents in the 2000 census*: "California City Prison
Gets $529 Million Federal Contract," www.ilovecalifornia
city.com/prison.html.

81   *federal contract to fill the beds with immigrants*: Corrections
Corporation of America, "California City Correctional Cen-

ter to Remain Open," press release, September 27, 2010, www.correctionscorp.com/newsroom/news-releases/226. On CCA's website (which looks a bit too much like a futuristic advertisement from the movie *Starship Troopers*), there is much pride in the rehabilitation programs. Yet for the life of me I cannot figure how to "rehabilitate" an immigrant.

81   *such as Arizona's controversial SB-1070*: Laura Sullivan, "Prison Economics Help Drive Arizona Immigration Law," National Public Radio, *Morning Edition*, October 28, 2010, www.npr.org/templates/story/story.php?storyId=130833741.

84   *medications when they were arrested*: Andrew P. Wilper, Steffie Woolhandler, J. Wesley Boyd, Karen E. Lasser, Danny McCormick, David H. Bor, and David U. Himmelstein, "The Health and Health Care of U.S. Prisoners: A Nationwide Survey," *American Journal of Public Health* 99, no. 4 (January 2009): 666–72.

86   *soon reached the general public*: Jennifer Gonnerman, "The Lost Boys of Tryon: Inside New York's most infamous juvenile prison, where troubled kids—abused and forgotten—learn to become troubled adults," *New York*, January 24, 2010.

87   *full-time psychiatrist on staff*: Gonnerman, "The Lost Boys of Tryon."

87   *"facilities all across the country."*: "Sentenced to Abuse," Editorial, *New York Times*, January 14, 2010.

87   *raped, mainly by staff members*: Allen J. Beck, Paige M. Harrison, and Paul Guerino, "Sexual Victimization in Juvenile Facilities Reported by Youth, 2008–09," US Department of Justice Bureau of Justice Statistics, January 2010.

87   *and suicide attempts are routine*: Nicholas Confessore, "A Glimpse Inside a Troubled Youth Prison," *New York Times*, February 12, 2010; Gonnerman, "The Lost Boys of Tryon."

88   *by the time they're twenty-eight*: Gonnerman, "The Lost Boys of Tryon."

91   *between a community and punishment*: Burrows and Wallace, *Gotham*, 367.

96   *"to be there, don't commit the crime."*: Richard Grant, "Banging Up the Bad Guys," *The Independent*, May 21, 1995, 6.

96   *deters crime or prevents recidivism*: John R. Hepburn and
      Marie L. Griffin, "Jail Recidivism in Maricopa County: A
      Report Submitted to the Maricopa County Sheriff's Office,"
      Maricopa County, AZ, 1998.

96   *doubled, to ten thousand prisoners*: Randal C. Archibold, "On
      Border Violence, Truth Pales Compared to Ideas," *New York
      Times*, June 19, 2010.

97   *Arpaio's policies garnered little hatred*: Marie L. Griffin, *The
      Use of Force by Detention Officers* (LFB Scholarly Publishing,
      2001), 44.

100   *back with the "cat-o'-nine-tails."*: *The Progress* (Clearfield, PA),
      March 8, 1972, cited in Hal Roth, "Old News from Del-
      marva: The Whipping Post in Maryland and Delaware,"
      Tidewater Times, July 2006, www.tidewatertimes.com/
      HalRothJuly2006.htm. In other accounts the flogged crim-
      inal is listed, probably erroneously, as a wife beater.

101   *"mode of whipping and pillory."*: *Delaware Gazette*, November
      11, 1853, 2.

101   *here's the kicker—"legal abstractions."*: Robert Graham Cald-
      well, *Red Hannah: Delaware's Whipping Post* (Philadelphia:
      University of Pennsylvania Press, 1947), 99.

104   *were now . . . a hell to me*: Mary W. Shelley, *Frankenstein, or
      The Modern Prometheus* (Boston: Sever, Francis, & Co.,
      1869), 45–46.

106   *meals to closing entire institutions*: *The Continuing Fiscal Crisis
      in Corrections: Setting a New Course*, Vera Institute of Justice,
      October 2010) www.vera.org/download?file=3072/The
      -continuing-fiscal-crisis-in-corrections-10-2010-updated
      .pdf.

107   *and communist Cuba (530)*: Ron Walmsley, *World Prison
      Population List*, 8th ed. (London: International Centre for
      Prison Studies, King's College, 2010). Nobody is certain
      about how many prisons are in North Korea, which may
      have a higher incarceration rate than America.

107   *five times the world's average*: Ron Walmsley, *World Prison
      Population List*. The world's incarceration rate is estimated
      at 150 per 100,000.

107   *from 60 to 110 per 100,000*: Charles A. Ellwood, "Has Crime
        Increased in the United States Since 1880?" *Journal of the
        American Institute of Criminal Law and Criminology* 1, no.
        3 (September 1910), 379.

110   *"imposes the punishment of flogging."*: Antonin Scalia, "Orig-
        inalism: The Lesser Evil," *University of Cincinnati Law Review*
        57 (1989): 849–66.

110   *"and not cruel and unusual, today."*: Stephen Breyer, *Making
        Our Democracy Work: A Judge's View* (New York: Knopf Dou-
        bleday, 2010).

120   *discretion, we make things worse*: Mandatory arrest for do-
        mestic violence became popular after the publication of the
        flawed Minneapolis Domestic Violence Experiment. But
        more recent experiments show the limitations of mandatory
        arrest and even mandatory prosecution. See Janell D.
        Schmidt and Lawrence W. Sherman, "Does Arrest Deter
        Domestic Violence?" *American Behavioral Scientist* 36 (1993):
        601–609; and Eve Buzawa and Aaron Buzawa, "Courting
        Domestic Violence Victims: A Tale of Two Cities," *Crimi-
        nology & Public Policy* 7, no. 4 (2008), 671–85.

124   *than a similar nonincarcerated person*: The Pew Charitable
        Trusts, *Collateral Costs: Incarceration's Effect on Economic Mo-
        bility* (Washington, DC: The Pew Charitable Trusts, 2010).

125   *and contrary to human rights law*: V. Sithambaram, *The Cur-
        rent Form of Sentencing Is Outdated: Time for Reform* (Kuala
        Lumpur: The Malaysian Bar, 2005), www.malaysianbar
        .org.my/criminal_law/the_current_form_of_sentencing_is_
        outdated_time_for_reform_by_v._sithambaram.html.

125   *flogs perhaps 16,000 people a year*: Amnesty International,
        "Malaysia: A Blow to Humanity: Torture by Judicial Caning
        in Malaysia," 2010, www.amnesty.org/en/library/info/ASA
        28/013/2010/en.

125   *canes more than 6,000 a year*: "Singapore," US Department
        of State, March 11, 2008, www.state.gov/g/drl/rls/hrrpt/
        2007/100537.htm.

125   *rate one-fourth of Singapore's*: Walmsley, *World Prison Popu-
        lation List*.

127   *The scars would never heal*: Robert Symes and Bob Hart, "In-
       side Story: In the Malaysian Prison System, Punishment
       Rarely Fits the Crime," from *Penthouse* (UK?), c. 1991,
       www.corpun.com/myjur1.htm. I was unable to locate this
       article. *Penthouse* has different publishers and editions in the
       United States, Australia, and the UK. My inquiries to two
       of the three houses (United States and Australia) failed to
       turn up the source. Further research is needed.

128   *There's a lot of pain*: "Michael Fay Interview on Larry King,"
       Larry King Live, June 29, 1994, cited at World Corporal
       Punishment Research, www.corpun.com/sgju9406.htm#4344.

129   *two-to-one support for his punishment*: Cyndi Banks, *Punish-
       ment in America: A Reference Handbook* (Santa Barbara, CA:
       ABC-CLIO, 2005), 139.

130   *asked in a few days to explain this system*: "Spanking by Elec-
       tricity: Kansas Has Invented a Method Which Colorado
       May Adopt," *New York Times*, February 14, 1898.

132   *widespread use of such devices*: Amnesty International, "USA:
       List of Deaths Following Use of Stun Weapons in US Law
       Enforcement: June 2001 to 31 August 2008," 2008, www
       .amnestyusa.org/uploads/ListOfDeaths.pdf. For an up-to-date
       list of Taser deaths, see Electronic Village, http://electronic
       village.blogspot.com/2009/05/taser-related-deaths-in-united
       -states.html.

140   *cost taxpayers £37 million (about $59 million)*: Steve Doughty,
       "£37Million: Huge Bill to the Taxpayer for Crimes of Just
       Two Families," *The Daily Mail*, July 22, 2010, 17, www.daily
       mail.co.uk/news/article-1296682/37MILLION-Huge
       -taxpayer-crimes-just-TWO-families.html.

142   *should be used to help real victims*: John Schmitt, Kris Warner,
       and Sarika Gupta, "The High Budgetary Cost of Incarcera-
       tion" (Washington, DC: Center for Economic and Policy
       Research, 2010).

147   *amputation, public stoning, or sharia law*: Though it may not
       help a defense of flogging, I should point out that Singapore-
       and Malaysian-style flogging is often much more severe than
       is generally practiced by Islamic extremists. The canings that
       occur under the guise of sharia law are typically administered

while maintaining a bent elbow, very much limiting the potential force. This stroke is more slapping than whipping. The purpose of these canings, often performed on clothed skin, is usually more about public shame than breaking the skin and causing pain.

152 *"a blinding moment of moral clarity."*: Kwame Anthony Appiah, "What Will Future Generations Condemn Us For?" *Washington Post*, September 26, 2010. See also Kwame Anthony Appiah, *The Honor Code: How Moral Revolutions Happen* (New York: Norton, 2010).

INDEX

SCASCO 24HJ5

Printed in the USA
CPSIA information can be obtained
at www.ICGtesting.com
LVHW030550300823
756700LV00004B/147